Modernism and the making of the Soviet New Man

Manchester University Press

Modernism and the making of the Soviet New Man

Tijana Vujošević

Manchester University Press

Copyright © Tijana Vujošević 2017

The right of Tijana Vujošević to be identified as the author of this work has been asserted by her in accordance with the Copyright, Designs and Patents Act 1988.

Published by Manchester University Press
Altrincham Street, Manchester M1 7JA, UK
www.manchesteruniversitypress.co.uk

British Library Cataloguing-in-Publication Data is available

ISBN 978 1 5261 1486 0 hardback
ISBN 978 1 5261 1488 4 paperback

First published by Manchester University Press in hardback 2017

This edition first published 2019

The publisher has no responsibility for the persistence or accuracy of URLs for any external or third-party internet websites referred to in this book, and does not guarantee that any content on such websites is, or will remain, accurate or appropriate.

Typeset by Toppan Best-set Premedia Limited, Hong Kong

Contents

List of figures *page* vii
List of tables xi
Acknowledgements xiii

Introduction 1
1 The will of the universe 11
2 Class unconsciousness 37
3 A home for a very industrious individual 65
4 The world in the bathhouse, the bathhouse in the world 97
5 Stalin and the housewife 125
6 Golden calf, golden tooth 155

Conclusion 177
Select bibliography 181
Index 189

Figures

1.1	Konstantin Tsiolkovsky, sketches no. 45–47 in "Album of Cosmic Journeys", made for the film "The Cosmic Voyage", 1932.	page 10
1.2	Konstantin Tsiolkovsky, sketch no. 29 from "Album of Cosmic Journeys" made for the film "The Cosmic Voyage", 1932.	13
1.3	Unknown photographer. Photo of Vladimir Tatlin inside the Letatlin, 1932.	22
1.4	Vladimir Tatlin, Letatlin, drawing, 1932.	23
1.5	The *Letatlin* on display in the State Museum of Fine Arts, Moscow, in 1932.	25
1.6	Attempts to Launch Vladimir Tatlin's Letatlin, Moscow, 1933.	25
1.7	"Comrades Stalin, Chkalov, Kaganovich, Ordzhonikidze and Belyakov on the Shchelkovo Airport in 1936."	28
1.8	Yuri Gagarin and Valentina Tereshkova feeding a tiger baby in Berlin, 1963.	29
1.9	Ilya Kabakov, "The Man who Flew into Space from His Apartment," Ronald Feldman Gallery, 1988. Courtesy of Emilia Kabakov.	31
1.10	Ilya Kabakov, "The Man who Flew into Space from His Apartment," exterior view. Courtesy of Emilia Kabakov.	32
2.1	Vsevolod Meyerhold, plan of scenic movement for "The Magnanimous Cuckold," 1922.	36

2.2	"Cyclogram of chopping wood with a chisel." Pedagogical Laboratory of the Central Institute of Labor, 1924.	41
2.3	"Bow and Arrow," biomechanical exercise.	47
2.4	"The Magnanimous Cuckold," poster with set design by Lyubov Popova, 1922.	52
2.5	"The Magnanimous Cuckold," set design by Lyubov Popova for the 1928 performance.	52
2.6	Lyubov Popova, costume for "The Magnanimous Cuckold," 1922.	54
2.7	*Chechotka*, in "The Magnanimous Cuckold" rehearsal of 1928.	55
2.8	Vsevolod Meyerhold, "Stella, Bruno, Florance, Wet Nurse" (plan of movement for the "Magnanimous Cuckold"), 1922.	56
2.9	Vsevolod Meyerhold, "Stella, Bruno, Nurse" (plan of movement for the "Magnanimous Cuckold"), 1922.	58
3.1	Petr Galaktionov, folding bed, 1923.	74
3.2	Nikolay Sobolev, bed-armchair, 1923.	75
3.3	Alexander Toporkov, furniture design.	75
3.4	Alexander Toporkov, sketch for a foldable bed.	76
3.5	Margarete Schütte-Lihotzky, Frankfurt kitchen, view.	79
3.6	Article on the rationalized kitchen in *Sovremennaya arkhitektura*, 1929.	80
3.7	Plans of the "ordinary kitchen", "rationalized kitchen," and "kitchen element" in *Sovremennaya arkhitektura*, 1929.	82
3.8	Vladimir Vladimirov and Mikhail Barshch, experimental project of a house-commune for the Typification Section of the Housing Commission of the RSFR, 1929.	83
3.9	"Sleeping cabin" (*spal'naya kabina*) in the house-commune by Vladimirov and Barshch, 1929.	84
3.10	Nikolay Milyutin, living cell (*zhilaya yacheyka*) in *Sotsgorod*, 1930.	86
3.11	Le Corbusier, Villa Savoye, Poissy, France, 1928–1931.	88
3.12	OSA, "Individual house no. 30," *Sovremennaya arkhitektura*, 1930.	89
3.13	"Individual House no. 30," facades and twelve plans, in *Sovremennaya arkhitektura*, 1930.	90
4.1	A group of men in the pool of the Trust for Public Baths and Laundries, Leningrad 1932.	96

List of figures ix

4.2	"Washing machine," *Problems of Municipal Economy*, 1931.	103
4.3	"Boiler and conveyor belt for laundries," *Problems of Municipal Economy*, 1931	104
4.4	Nikolay Demkov, *Banya* on 3 Stantsionnaya Street, c. 1930 (photo 1934).	105
4.5	Alexander Gegello: Sanitary Conveyer of the Vasileostrovsky District, 1931.	106
4.6	Gegello and Krichevsky, "Design for a crematorium," *Problems of Municipal Economy*, 1930.	108
4.7	Alexander Nikolsky, project for a bathhouse, unbuilt, original drawing, 1927.	110
4.8	Alexander Nikolsky, project for a bathhouse, the design that was built in 1930.	112
4.9	Nikolsky, "Round Bathhouse," *USSR in Construction*, no. 11 (Nov.) 1931.	113
4.10	Kazimir Malevich, *House under Construction*, 1915.	115
4.11	Ilya Chashnik, Suprematist Arkhitekton with Central Nucleus, 1928.	116
4.12	Anatoly Ladinsky, "Bath in Tyumen," *Stroitelstvo Moskvy*, 1932.	118
4.13	Bath in Tyumen, scheme of the bathing sequence. Author's sketch.	119
5.1	Young mother votes at the labour ward for the best friend of working women and children, comrade Stalin, *Obshchestvennitsa*, 1938.	124
5.2	Women reading *Obshchestvennitsa* together, *Obshchestvennitsa*, 1938.	126
5.3	Jabot and jackets, *Obshchestvennitsa*, 1937.	128
5.4	Ads for face creams "Flora" and "Onyx," *Obshchestvennitsa*, 1938.	129
5.5	Peter Paul Rubens. *Holy Family with the Basket*, 1616, reprinted in *Obshchestvennitsa* 1, 1936.	130
5.6.	Untitled (child), in *Obshchestvennitsa*, 1937.	132
5.7	Arkady Plastov, *Feast on a Collective Farm*, 1937. © Arkadij Aleksandrovich Plastov/ADAGP. Licensed by Viscopy, 2016.	134
5.8	Side cabinet (buffet) in a nursery, *Obshchestvennitsa*, 1936.	136

5.9	Fountain in the mechanical department of a train depot, *Obshchestvennitsa*, 1938.	139
5.10	Wife-activists of the Debaltsev station creating a flower garden in front of the passenger platform, *Obshchestvennitsa*, 1937.	140
5.11	"Before" image of a factory dining hall, *Obshchestvennitsa*, 1938.	141
5.12	"After" image of a factory dining hall, *Obshchestvennitsa*, 1938.	142
5.13	Civil defence class, *Obshchestvennitsa*, 1937.	145
5.14	Driving classes wearing gas masks, *Obshchestvennitsa*, 1937.	146
5.15	Activists of the oil plant in the name of Kaganovich (in Baku) finishing their training mission in gas masks. *Obshchestvennitsa*, 1937.	149
6.1	Brigadier Rebrov, Lenin Medallist, in *How We Built the Metro*, 1935.	154
6.2.	Workers' parade on the day of Metro opening, 15 May 1935, in *How We Built the Metro*.	158
6.3	Celebration at the House of Soviets 14 May 1935, in *How We Built the Metro*.	159
6.4	Krasnoselskaya station, in *How We Built the Metro*.	160
6.5	Ceiling of Lenin Library station, in *How We Built the Metro*.	160
6.6	Capitol at Komsomolskaya station, in *How We Built the Metro*.	165
6.7	Likhtenberg and Dushkin, Dvorets Sovetov station (renamed "Kropotkinskaya") in *Stroitelstvo Moskvy*, 1935.	166
6.8	Inspection of metro cars, in *How We Built the Metro*.	168
6.9	Dzerzhinsky Square station, entry hall, in *How We Built the Metro*.	170
6.10	Shock workers resting, in *How We Built the Metro*.	171
6.11	The labour of our party is our literature: our combat and our Revolutionary work, in *How We Built the Metro*.	172
6.12	Mosaic at Komsomolskaya station, in *How we Built the Metro*.	172

Tables

3.1 Stanislav Strumilin, "Leisure Time in the Worker's Family – Monthly Budget in Hours per Worker," originally in *Voprosy Truda* (*Labor Issues*) no. 3–4, 1923. Translated by author. *page* 64

3.2 Stanislav Strumilin, "Domestic Labor in the Households of Office Workers in 1923–24 (in the number of hours per worker per month)," first published in *Planovoe khozyaystvo* (*Planned Economy*) no. 8, 1925, excerpt. Translated by author. 67

3.3 Stanislav Strumilin, "Domestic Inventory of Workers in December of 1923 Classified by Material," originally published in *Statistiko-ekonomicheskie etyudy* (*Statistico-economic Studies*), 1926. Translated by author. 71

Acknowledgements

I would like to thank mentors and colleagues with whom I shared ideas about this research and who read the manuscript in various stages of development: Mark Jarzombek, Erika Naginski, Elizabeth Wood, Alla Vronskaya, Igor Demchenko, Fabiola Lopez-Duran, Shundana Yusaf, Anatoly Rykov, Mitya Kozlov, Deborah Kully, Mechtild Widrich, Michael Osman, Bill Taylor, Darren Jorgensen, Iva Glisic, Mark Edele, Danilo Udovicki-Selb, as well as the editorial teams at *Grey Room*, *Architectural Histories*, and *Journal of Design History*, where some of this material was previously published. Lenore Hietkamp played a key role in crafting the final version of the text. Finally, and most importantly, I thank the team at Manchester University Press for their patience, insight, and commitment.

By focusing my study on the construction of this New Man I depart from an established paradigm. For the most part, historians have considered collective spaces as the unique product of Soviet design. These include collective houses (*dom-kommuny*), as imagined by the constructivist OSA group and realized in buildings such as the Narkomfin block of apartments by Ginzburg and Milinis; workers' clubs, such Melnikov's Rusakov club;[8] or the visionary architecture from the early 1920s, which remained on paper. Accordingly, Soviet designs were seen as designs for the collective, for the masses. Communist designs were, in fact, not only designs for collective life. The prerequisite for articulating group identities is the identity of the basic social "unit" – the socialist individual. Designing this individual, as well as designing *for* him or her, was an ideological and practical task that defined Soviet architecture of the 1920s and the 1930s.

The notion that the history of modernity can be explored as the history of the self is far from new. It particularly dominates French post-structuralism and the critical theory of the 1990s influenced by it in the English language. Critics of modern society have written sophisticated and groundbreaking analyses of how literature, speech, and everyday rituals shape the protagonist of modern life.[9] The main question this line of inquiry poses is that of agency: to what extent men and women of the modern age are fashioned or constrained by the dominant system of values and beliefs promoted by those in power, and to what extent their choices are free. This question of freedom is never outdated.

This approach is especially appropriate in my study of a culture whose main and openly stated goal was the creation of a new kind of human being. I will look at how the material environment was shaped and conceptualized with the intent to forge this New Man. Through a series of case studies, I present Soviet architecture – the nexus between utopia and reality, power and individual agency – as episodic history. These case studies span consecutive but radically different political, aesthetic, and economic milieus – the New Economic Policy, followed by the Five-Year Plans. Historians have come up with a variety of ways to distinguish between these periods. One is to summarily characterize the new Economic Policy, or "Leninism," as utopian and the period of the Five-Year Plans, or "Stalinism," as totalitarian. Another is to distinguish the internationalism of the Soviet early years from the radical nationalism of "socialism in one country" under Stalin's rule. An important contribution to this chronology is Paperny's classic study that identifies "Leninist" and "Stalinist" architecture as the product of two cultural mechanisms at work in the 1920s and the 1930s respectively.[10] An exceptionally original and fruitful approach to the history of the early Soviet era is that of Katerina Clark, who explores the two periods in terms of their paradigmatic metropolitan cultures, that of Leningrad and that of Moscow.[11]

In this book I will build upon Dobrenko's theory of Stalinism as a society in which images and representations mediate all social and economic relations.[12] My interpretation of Soviet architecture as an identity-making enterprise is based on a loose interpretation of this theory, according to which the 1920s were essentially productivist and 1930s essentially representational. As this book establishes, in the 1920s Soviet power was meant to be power over means of production, while in the 1930s it was the power of demonstrating (by means of art, architecture, design, popular culture, science) the value of socialism in one country. Case studies in this book demonstrate the notion that architecture of the 1920s defined the New Man as primarily a worker. In contrast, during the 1930s the New Man was supposed to be an admirer of socialism in aesthetic terms – the "connoisseur" of socialism as a *gesamtkunstwerk*, the total work of art created by the Communist Party.

The boundaries between the two eras are not always sharp, especially in the case of architecture, which changes slowly and involves delays between conceptualization and realization. I am taking these deferments and anachronisms into account as I traverse the tumultuous period of the post-Revolutionary decades. In Chapter 1, "The will of the universe," I set the stage for discussing this historical course by providing an overview of the evolution of Soviet subjectivity. The lens for exploring this development is the ultimate symbol of the journey towards communism – narratives about the conquest of the skies and concepts of "outer space" as the physical realm in which the New Man will come into being. Chapters 2 and 3, "Class unconsciousness" and "A home for the very industrious individual," are dedicated to the role of architecture in promoting a productivist ethos. In the 1920s the working class formed only a small fraction of the overall population, and enlightened, "class conscious" workers – the proletarians – were a tiny minority. The task of architecture, I posit, was to create the proletarian. Proposals for a truly socialist environment were intended to impart the idea that labour was not only an economic activity but also the meaning of all existence. Two case studies reveal how space and the material environment defined the New Man: Vsevolod Meyerhold's designs for a biomechanical stage, based on the theories of scientific organization of labour; and domestic "instruments" designed for the proletarian home.

The transition from the productivist ethos of the 1920s to the representational ethos of the 1930s is epitomized in the public baths constructed around 1930 in Leningrad and Moscow, discussed in the Chapter 4, "The world in the bathhouse, the bathhouse in the world." These structures were envisioned as both efficient machines for the production of cleanliness and microcosmic representations of the Soviet society. Chapter 5, "Stalin and the housewife," presents a particular genre of socialist realism – the environmental expertise of *obshchestvennitsy*, or socially minded women. These were housewives from provincial industrial towns who translated the aesthetic of socialist realist painting and official rhetoric about the "joyous" world of socialism into an aesthetic for home and garden – an attempt to transform the intimate world into a masterpiece of socialist realism.

Soviet architecture evolved over the course of the 1920s and the 1930s from a productivist to a representational enterprise. This evolution was also a process in which architecture became less and less abstract; a process in which, with the consolidation of state power, conceptual projects were replaced by built structures. While this book begins with a story about celestial imagination and the conquest of the ether, it ends with a project for a space below ground, the Moscow Metro which opened in 1935, the most colossal Soviet public work. The final Chapter 6, "Golden calf, golden tooth," explores the history of this immense structure, clad in expensive marble and illuminated by electrical lighting, altogether the embodiment of socialist modernity. The process of its construction was meant to transform its builders, peasants coming from all parts of the Soviet Union, into New Men – enlightened urbanites. These men and women were not only record-breaking workers but also experts on socialist beauty, and they elaborated upon their political and aesthetic expertise in a blockbuster propaganda volume, *How We Built the Metro*.

Projects of the 1920s and the 1930s forged the Soviet New Man by providing settings and aesthetic templates for the personal and the everyday. Their study contributes to the understanding of early Soviet cultural history and the evolving ethos of modernism, of which Soviet architecture is the most radical manifestation. This ethos, both idealistic and pragmatic, both sublime and mundane, has not been pursued in a singular way in the history of Soviet, but also Western, modernism. The different manifestations of this ethos explored in this book shed light on the horizons, limitations, and fate of the ultimate modernist attempt to use art to execute a political and social overhaul.

Notes

1 The interpretation of Soviet intellectual and cultural history as utopian dominates Western scholarship. In historical literature, it was established by Richard Stites. Stites' seminal work, *Revolutionary Dreams: Utopian Vision and Experimental Life in the Soviet Union* (Oxford University Press, 1988), traces the origins of what he calls Russian "social daydreaming" in the nineteenth-century Russian visionary tradition, for example in Chernishevsky's *What Is to Be Done?*, or, in the populist movement, the mystical works of Fedorov, Tsiolkovsky's and Bogdanov's Cosmism, and others. Stites' *Revolutionary Dreams* laid the groundwork for the possibility of interpreting Soviet history not as an isolated communist experiment, nor merely as an attempt to implement Marxist ideas, but as an extension of pre-Revolutionary tradition that involved translating Western social visions. Stites' use of the notions of "utopia" and "dreaming" establishes a narrative according to which the cries for social reform were pure and lofty from the nineteenth century to the 1920s and according to which it was Stalinist terror that led to the perversion of these ideas and their utilization by the totalitarian cause.
2 In the field of architecture, the most important interpretation of this narrative about lofty ideals and their demise during the "bloody" epoch of "Stalinism" is Hugh Hudson's popular book with the dramatic title *Blueprints and Blood: The Stalinization of Soviet Architecture* (Princeton University Press, 1993; 2015). It describes how Stalinist forces within the architectural profession suffocated the avant-garde, thus engaging in "terror from below" that preceded and announced the years of Great Terror.
3 The earliest comprehensive Western exhibition of Russian avant-garde art, planned as a new kind of collaboration between the East and the West at the very end of Soviet socialism, was organized by the Russian Museum and the Tretyakov Gallery in collaboration with the Guggenheim Museum and The Frankfurt Schirn Kunsthalle. The exhibition, entitled "The Great Utopia," toured Germany, the Netherlands, and the USA in 1992. In the introduction to the thick volume that accompanied it, the curators explain that their initial working title, "Construction and Intuition," which referred to the aesthetic principles and processes that defined the Soviet avant-garde, was changed to the final title by their "Western colleagues." This change of

title, and of the entire conceptualization of the avant-garde as a utopian movement, stemmed from the need to confront the relationship between the politics and the artistic legacy of the Soviet Union. The presentation of Russian avant-garde art as utopian is introduced in the catalogue by Thomas Krens, the Guggenheim administrator, and Michael Govan, and it articulates a narrative that mirrors that of Stites. Like the Russian revolutionaries of October, avant-garde artists are, according to these authors, "idealistic," their plans working well in theory but badly in practice. In the 1930s, when art was connected with political practice – "instrumentalised," the authors say – utopia and idealism ended.

4 The separation of radical and progressive revolutionary goals from revolutionary violence characterizes the work of authors contributing to the art history journal *October*. In the period spanning the 1980s to recent years, this separation has allowed the authors to identify with the 1920s revolutionaries while not fundamentally challenging the liberal democratic art historical discourse they participate in. In 1984, Benjamin Buchloh published the most influential article of this kind, "From faktura to factography," which clearly separated Leninism from Stalinism in aesthetic terms in *October* 30 (Autumn 1984): 82–119. More recently, Kristina Kiaer, who studies the Soviet notion of the object, published "Boris Arvatov's socialist objects" in *October* 81 (Summer 1997): 105–118, which she expanded into the full-length manuscript: *Imagine No Possessions* (MIT Press, 2005). The work of *October* raised awareness of the importance of the Soviet project. But the notion that Soviet art of the 1920s can be used as a template for resistance is suspect because of the radical difference in social context between then and now and the radically different understanding of means for achieving political goals.

5 The boundary between the 1920s and the 1930s in the realm of art and architecture is not as clear cut as American leftist criticism would have it. Consider, for example, the well-documented work of El Lissitsky on the 1930s propaganda magazine *USSR in Construction*. Even more convincing is Danilo Udovički-Selb's paradigm-changing discussion of the continuity of modernist architecture in the 1930s ("Between modernism and socialist realism: Soviet Architectural culture during Stalin's revolution from above, 1928–1938," *Journal of the Society of Architectural Historians* 68 no. 4 (December 2009): 467–495). As Udovički-Selb points out, the delay from conception to execution in architecture challenges the notion of synchronicity between political upheaval and transformations of the built environment. This is even more true in the case of everyday buildings, such as bathhouses, bakeries, and schools, which were often modernist throughout the 1930s. The explanation for this lack of synchronicity is that, while reflecting major political overhauls, architecture also belongs to the realm of what Braudel

defined as the "longue durée," the slow change of the material environment and everyday habits.

6 In the *Total Art of Stalinism: Aesthetic Dictatorship and Beyond* (1988; Princeton: Princeton University Press, 1992; London: Verso Books, 2011), Boris Groys goes even further than establishing the sharp contrast between the 1920s and the 1930s, during which progressive ideals of the avant-garde were presumably betrayed. According to him, and to the circle of Moscow conceptual artists to which he belonged, the art of socialist realism developed upon an avant-garde foundation. Furthermore, the Stalinist political project is the ultimate realization of totalizing avant-garde aspirations.

7 The radical leftist tradition of architectural history claims that the capitalist avant-garde is utopian as well, drawing on the examples of "paper architecture"; that is, unbuilt designs. The most famous instance of this is the criticism of Manfredo Tafuri who, in his seminal works *Architecture and Utopia* (1973; Cambridge: MIT Press, 1976) and *The Sphere and the Labyrinth* (1980; Cambridge MIT Press, 1990), establishes that the work of Giovanni Battista Piranesi, which existed only on paper, marks the beginning of a utopian tradition which reflects the inherent contradictions of the capitalist order and the ultimate impossibility of producing social change within it. Capitalist designs share with those in the communist society the fundamental modern paradox: that effecting political change demands collaboration with the State and a betrayal of any ideological purity – if it existed in the first place. In this respect, it would follow that avant-garde "experiments," like successful "bourgeois" projects, demanded a pact with power for their realization, and that the notion that the avant-garde reached its apex in Stalinism might not be entirely ludicrous.

8 The connection between Soviet art and the Soviet State is usually examined in terms of how architecture attempted to serve the collectivist ideals of the Communist Party. See, for example, Anatole Kopp, *Town and Revolution: Soviet Architecture and City Planning 1917–1935*, trans. Thomas E. Burton (London: Thames and Hudson, 1970); Selim Omarovich Han-Magomedov, *Pioneers of Soviet Architecture: The Search for New Solutions in the 1920s and the 1930s*, trans. Alexander Lieven, ed. Catherine Cooke (London: Thames and Hudson, 1987); and Andrey Ikonnikov, *Russian Architecture of the Soviet Period*, trans. Lev Ljapin (London: Collets, 1988). This perspective has been recently adopted in Jean-Louis Cohen's textbook, *The Future of Architecture since 1889: A Worldwide History* (Phaidon, 2012).

9 The realization of collectivist ideals would be impossible without first defining the communist individual. The groundwork for the study of subjectivity in Western cultural theory has been established by Louis Althusser, Jaques Lacan, Michel Foucault, Gilles Deleuze, Felix Guattari, and Jacques Rancière. Despite numerous and sophisticated differences, including radically

different opinions on individual agency, these theorists all believe that the terms of discourse and representation fundamentally define who an individual is or is not. Battles over defining the identity of the citizen are key both for the operation of power and the struggle for freedom. Architecture, as the nexus between aesthetics and everyday ritual, plays a key role in the design of self – in the design of citizens as political beings.

10 Vladimir Paperny, in *Architecture in the Age of Stalin: Culture Two* (1985; Cambridge: Cambridge University Press, 2002, 2011), defines the difference in the architectures and protagonists of the two big historical periods, "Stalinism" and "Leninism," as the difference between two cultures. To Paperny, the two periods are characterized by cultural changes that resemble natural phenomena, created not only by power but by all participants in the Soviet social intercourse. Soviet history, Paperny says, is the product of dichotomies such as those of movement and immobility, uniformity and hierarchy, the lyrical and the epic.

11 The difference between the cultures of the 1920s and the 1930s that Paperny described in terms of broad and abstract dichotomies is explored by Katerina Clark in *Petersburg, Crucible of the Cultural Revolution* (Cambridge: Harvard University Press, 1995) and *Moscow the Fourth Rome: Stalinism, Cosmopolitanism and the Evolution of Soviet Culture, 1931–1941* (Cambridge: Harvard University Press, 2011). She captures the complexity of the social, cultural, and political space of pre-War Soviet history by tying it to two cities which serve not only as material environments but also crucibles for distinct sets of ideas about Russian destiny. Clark challenges common assumptions about the contrast between the 1920s and the 1930s, including those of Paperny and his Moscow circle. According to her nuanced account, the pre-War Stalinist age which, Paperny would say, was the inflexible and petrified system of hierarchical and historicist ideas that replaced the revolutionary 1920s, is more complex and heterogeneous and involves internationalist and avant-garde currents alongside or even within a conservative and totalitarian discourse.

12 For the purposes of this book, a study of the role of architecture in articulating the identity of Soviet citizen as a truly communist being, the best theoretical framework is that outlined by Evgeny Dobrenko in his *Political Economy of Socialist Realism* (New Haven: Yale University Press, 2007). Dobrenko's study is less a description of the Soviet self, however, and more a study of the ways in which that self was created. Dobrenko's book presents two theses that are also crucial for my study. The first is that advertising, science, statistics, and administrative documents can be examined as aesthetic practices. The second is that aesthetic practices not only represent reality but also play a key role in shaping it.

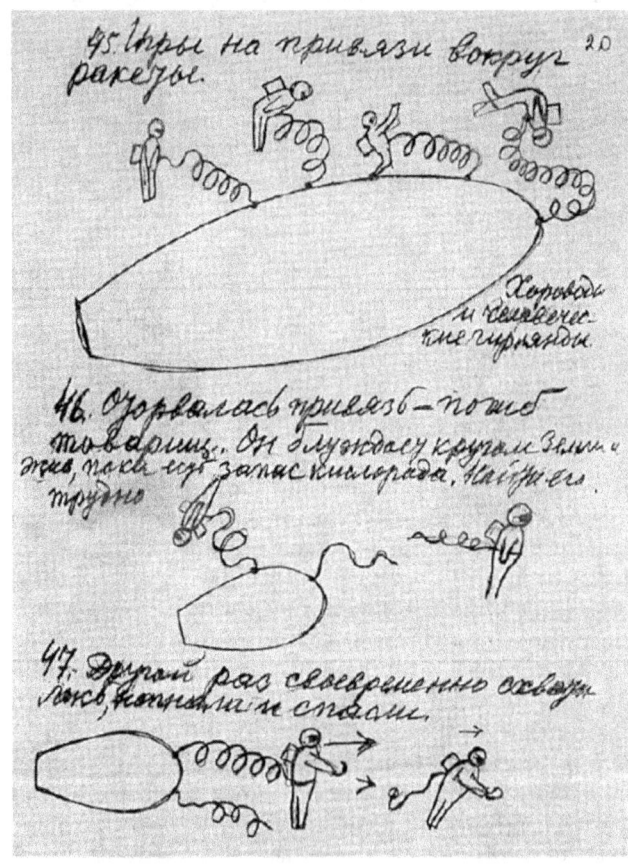

1.1 Konstantin Tsiolkovsky, sketches no. 45–47 in "Album of Cosmic Journeys," made for the film "The Cosmic Voyage," 1932.

1

The will of the universe

The cosmic voyage

A group of cosmonauts float in outer space, tethered to their spaceship, in a series of crudely rendered sketches. The handwriting accompanying the sketch, the first of three on a page (Figure 1.1), explains that life in space involves "playing games around the spaceship," and forming "human garlands." In the two sketches beneath the garland, play is replaced by celestial drama. The hose connecting one cosmonaut breaks and his body drifts away from the ship. He is dead, the note explains. But in the third scene, an arrow points from the eyes and hands of a tethered cosmonaut toward the one floating in space. In an alternative scenario, the explanation tells us, a fellow cosmonaut reacts in a timely manner to the mishap and manages to save his "comrade."

These numbered sketches are part of a series of drawings from the notebook of the scientist Konstantin Tsiolkovsky, prepared for the film *Cosmic Voyage*. In addition to presenting in his drawings cosmic pleasures, perils, and camaraderie, Tsiolkovsky also laid the foundations for Russian space travel. At least half a century before the Soviet Union launched its cosmonauts, he produced technical inventions that made Russian victories in the Space Race possible. Over the course of fifty years, from the end of the nineteenth century to the beginning of the twentieth, Tsiolkovsky developed visions of life in the universe and calculated ways to attain that life. He had survived the tsarist regime, witnessed the Revolution of 1917, lived during the era of Lenin's New Economic Policy of the 1920s, and finally seen the beginning of Stalin's Five-Year Plans, all the while spending most of his time in the little village of Kaluga,

200 kilometres from Moscow. In his teens, during a three-year stay in Moscow, he learned mathematics, physics, astronomy, and chemistry from books borrowed from public libraries.[1] The other source of his self-education was the work of Jules Verne. Relying on textbooks and Verne, this visionary created a mathematical model of liquid-propelled rockets, without which the Soviet space programme of the 1960s would have been impossible. Tsiolkovsky, a scientific amateur by common standards, operated from a homemade lab, and during the tsarist era supported himself by writing popular science for members of amateur space travel societies. During the Stalinist period, several years before his death, he finally received official recognition as a national hero.

Tsiolkovsky wanted to provide a comprehensive design for the space mission. He designed the first working rockets, but also items such as picture windows through which, as one of his sketches shows, naked women floating in space could look at the stars (Figure 1.2). He provided not just the know-how for launching a rocket into space, but also a body of metaphysical thought to accompany it. For Tsiolkovsky, everything that exists is driven by an entity he calls "the will of the universe." In a book with this phrase as its title, he explains the purpose of his life's work.[2] Human history, he proposes, is part of a trans-human evolution of the cosmos, driven by a transcendental power that is not absolute and immutable but evolves as it drives history. Today, this power, "the will of the universe," reveals itself "as the will of an unreasonable being."[3] Since the transcendental power in the world is still irrational, Tsiolkovsky writes,

> we see the mixture of sensible and stupid, kind and cruel in the affairs of the earth and mankind. What is the sense of poverty, diseases, prisons, malice, wars, death, stupidity, ignorance, narrow-mindedness of science, earthquakes, hurricanes, bad harvests, droughts, floods, vermin, ferocious animals, bad climate, etc?.[4]

But humankind evolves together with the cosmic will, toward greater perfection, toward self-empowerment, toward a "glorious state."[5] It will reach this state when it starts exploring the solar system or moves to some other system in the Milky Way and finds that single planet in which are "more favorable conditions for the development of higher intelligence." As the "will" evolves, humankind conquers the "Ether" and "liquidates painlessly everything imperfect, populating planets with a perfect generation."[6]

The will of the universe

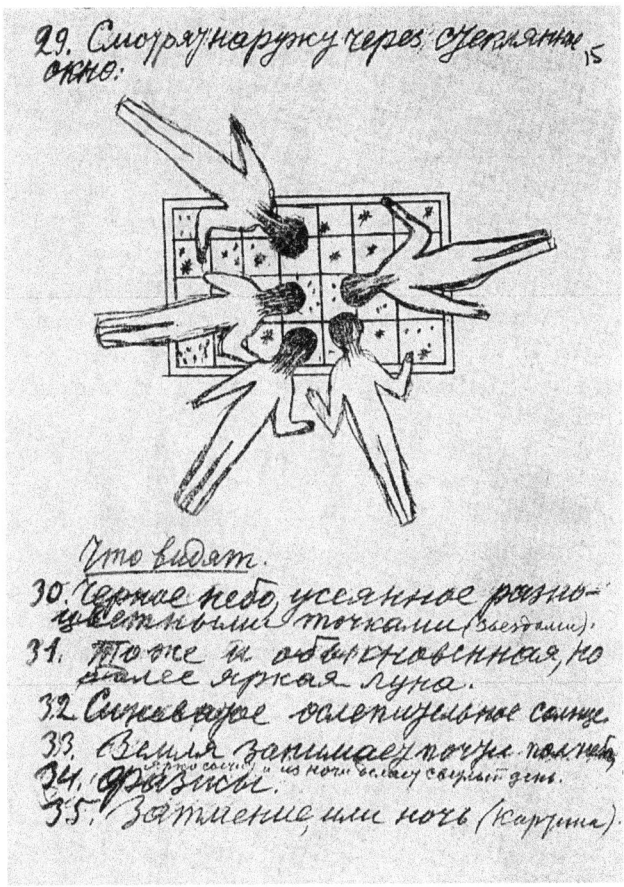

1.2 Konstantin Tsiolkovsky, sketch no. 29 from "Album of Cosmic Journeys" made for the film "The Cosmic Voyage", 1932.

In 1928, the year *The Will of the Universe* was published, the era of Stalin's Five-Year Plans began. In this context, Tsiolkovsky's reasoning about the nature of human progress and the celestial destination of the human race fits into the communist master narrative. It matches the teaching that first there is socialism, an evolutionary stage on the path toward the end of history, and communism is this history's end, a perfect classless and stateless society in which the imperfections of the human race and the "mixture of sensible and stupid, kind and cruel" will finally vanish. Tsiolkovsky's work on situating communism in outer space and presenting the path toward life in it as the manifestation of a cosmic will in many ways lends the communist master-narrative a transcendental dimension, and presents the course of Soviet history as part of cosmic evolution.

Tsiolkovsky's celestial utopia is situated in outer space – the metaphysical milieu of the cosmic void. To picture this void, to invent the means for reaching it, means not only to design an alternative reality, but also to speculate about the ends of human existence and the meaning of history. What does this mean in the context of socialist speculation? What form does a celestial utopia take when a religious interpretation of the heavens is replaced with a socialist one? How did projects such as Tsiolkovsky's, or, as later chapters explore, projects which pair the realistic with the fantastic, the far-reaching vision with the ridiculous, articulate the metaphysics of communism? How do the instigators of such projects speak about history or about the ends of communism as the radical modernist effort to transform the world? A good way to begin considering answers to these questions is to look precisely at the tradition of cosmic and celestial utopias – the most literal version of communist metaphysics – from their origins in pre-Revolutionary science and fiction and up to their concluding chapter at the end of Soviet history.

Communism and the Martians

The work of the rocket engineer and designer of "human garlands" belongs to the cosmist movement, which emerged in the decades before the October Revolution and was based on the work of late nineteenth-century theologian Nikolay Fedorov. Fedorov promoted the idea that the "common mission" of mankind was eternal life and the conquest of space. People inspired by Fedorov claimed that fundamental human rights included the right to eternal life and the right to interplanetary travel, both of which demanded liberation from capitalism. In addition to Tsiolkovsky, members of this group included such influential figures as Leonid Krasin, the designer of the Lenin Mausoleum, and Valerian Muravev, a writer and philosopher, one of the managers of the Central Institute of Labour founded to improve production efficiency. Writing about training factory workers in the Central Institute of Labour, Muravev combined ideas about efficient production with ideas about immortality. Like the director of the Institute, Aleksey Gastev, whose work will be discussed in Chapter 2, Muravev believed that the rhythm of factory work has to be synchronized with that of the cosmos; at that point the proletariat will eliminate the earthly notion of time and begin to live in the celestial eternal present.

The most popular pre-Revolutionary book that presents revolutionary life as celestial life is Alexander Bogdanov's *Red Star*, published in 1908. Bogdanov, one of the founders of the Russian Social Democratic Labour Party from which the Bolsheviks and the Soviet Communist Party descended, decided to popularize the proletarian struggle. So he wrote an adventure story in which the protagonist travels to the ideal communist society in space. Martians, led by an undercover agent named Menni, select the hero of the story, Leonid, a member of the Russian Socialist Democratic Party, to visit Mars so he can report back to the humans about what he learns. He travels via an "etheroneph" powered by "antimatter" and observes daily life on the Red Planet. He sees factories in which workers indulge in fulfilling labour and are free to change professions; fantastic glass-clad domestic architecture; progressive ways of childrearing; free love; and art museums transformed from sites for collection and accumulation into places for study. By experiencing everyday life in a Martian society, Leonid gets a picture of what his political struggle on Earth will bring about.

In one scene in the novel, Leonid admires the beauty of vegetation on Mars, which is all red because of a red substance that resembles chlorophyll.

> "Red is the colour of our socialist banner," I [Leonid] said. "So I shall simply have to get used to your socialist vegetation."
>
> "In that case you must also recognize the presence of socialism in the plants on Earth," Menni remarked. "Their leaves also possess a red hue, but it is concealed by the stronger [capitalist?] green colour. If you were to don a pair of glasses which completely absorb the green waves of light but admit the red ones, you would see that your forests and fields are as red as ours."[7]

By describing the minutiae of everyday life on Mars, Bogdanov narrates life in communism as a parallel space odyssey, making communism tangible and popularizing it in much the same way that Tsiolkovsky renders the outcome of his cosmic pursuits by sketching the life of cosmonauts. Bogdanov's text reveals the purpose of this process of rendering utopian life. He wants to create "glasses which completely absorb the green waves of light" and have the reader recognize in the present historical moment the origins of a society that may be fictional, existing only in an imagined outer space, but whose story is a lens for recognizing the potential of the present. It is a fiction that is intended to drive history.

Bogdanov's text about "red glasses" is about recognizing that communism is possible, but the notion of "red glasses" can also refer to the novel itself. *Red Star* was a vehicle for inciting communist passions and the desire to turn Earth from a green planet into a red one. The transcendental power that drives social change – what Tsiolkovksy would call "the will of the universe" – is materialized in science fiction, the kind of science fiction that, as Marx would put it, is meant "not only to interpret the world but to change it." Neither cosmist narratives nor their most ambitious and exuberant genre, pre-Revolutionary science fiction, could be called daydreams. Not only did they describe alternative ways of life but they were also used as a tool by which real-life proponents of those alternative ways of life wanted to propel history towards those alternatives. Such narratives were intended both to describe life in utopia and to explain the celestial inevitability of social transformation.

A socialist utopia, cosmism included, is almost by definition a collectivist utopia, consisting of propositions for replacing capitalist individualism with an enlightened collectivism as the expression of scientific, technical, and ethical progress. In fact, cosmist utopias involved new visions of collectivity. In *The Will of the Universe* Tsiolkovsky writes that "in a more considerable interval of time our Solar system will be densely populated and governed by an elected council," and that "all the other planets and solar systems will also unite"[8] into a union perhaps analogous to that of the Communist International. Bogdanov was a believer in "physiological collectivism," which involved people not only connecting spiritually but becoming one big organism by exchanging bodily fluids. Bogdanov wrote *Red Star* before the Revolution; after the Revolution, in 1926, he founded, under state tutelage, an Institute of Blood Transfusions to create a massive exchange of blood that was to ultimately render Russians immortal, and tried to convince the general public to accept this idea.[9] He died two years later, after exchanging a litre of blood with a student infected by malaria and tuberculosis, falling prey to his own imaginative collectivist scheme.

But the idea that socialist utopia is exclusively about collectivism, or that the best way to understand it is to look at what kind of collectives it proposes, has to be reconsidered. To understand the celestial collectivity, one has to start with the representations of the celestial individual – the comrade cruising the skies and travelling towards utopia – for it is of these individuals that the collectivity consists.

A complex representation of the communist revolutionary can be found in *Red Star*. The novel describes the Martian community and, through Leonid's story, all the drama and agony inherent in the project of understanding and creating such a community. On his visit to Mars, Leonid cannot process all the impressions, falls ill, and begins hallucinating. Upon recovering, he learns that the Martians are entertaining the idea of killing people on Earth to colonize it, because they think that most Earthlings cannot embrace communist principles. This frightens Leonid, who murders the Martian mastermind of this project and is finally returned to Earth. Our hero ends up in a psychiatric hospital. He is not certain whether he really went to Mars, or whether the entire trip is imagined. But then, in a twist, he is visited again by his Martian friends and given a second chance.

In the story, the ideal citizen of utopia, who is the celestial Martian, meets the confused and fragile man of the Earth, who is not yet ready for communism or revolution. Although he is offered a vivid experience of this new way of living, he fails both as a communist and as a harbinger of the communist message to the world. He is unable to withstand the glimpse of a life of the future, and cannot accept violence as means of transforming the world. Leonid has to personally transform, to become a new man capable of leading the revolution and a member of what Tsiolkovsky would call the "perfect generation."

The work of cosmists, and in particular Tsiolkovsky's phantasmagoria of life in outer space and Bogdanov's science fiction, as odd as they might be, render the political idea of spiritual and cultural transformation of the Russian society more tangible, more real, more easily comprehended. Cosmists' efforts to present scenes from utopian life inevitably produced not only a picture of a new ethical and political order but also a picture of concrete material environments, the devices for inhabiting them, and the revolutionary individual who would finally live according to "the will of the universe." Ultimately, according to authors of cosmic utopias, Russia was in the process of becoming a socialist society with a proper place in the universe, engaged in the pursuit of both international communism and interplanetary exchange.

"The Winged Sage"

Just prior to the October Revolution of 1917, and for a short while after it, celestial mythology became the main instrument for articulating ideas about social change, the Revolution, and revolutionary identity. The vehicles for reaching the communist utopia were, instead of "eteronephs," more modest and more practical devices – aeroplanes. In the 1910s, aeroplanes were becoming a symbol of both technological and political progress and signalled hope that the tsarist regime would come to an end. People gathered to see plane demonstrations in Moscow, Saint Petersburg, and Odessa, and followed the pilots' feats with fascination.[10] The visitors at demonstrations were not the well-to-do but small-time merchants, workers, and the urban poor. For them, the appearance of aeroplanes and the fantastic launch of man into the skies announced change, the promise that social tyranny, closely linked to technological backwardness, would be destroyed. A myth of the aeroplane emerged, in which planes and pilots were compared to characters from traditional epic poetry. People considered a pilot the contemporary version of an epic knight (*bogatir*). One aeroplane, for instance, was called "Russian Bogatyr," and another "Ilya Muromets" after the popular medieval hero who fought the Eastern hordes. The tsarist regime understood this dimension of the demonstrations, so it banned the import of aeroplanes and aeroplane parts, and all members of flight clubs had to register with the police.

Popular fascination with aeroplanes was reflected in the work of Russian futurists. In a treatise published in 1918, the futurist revolutionary is split between the earthly and the celestial self. Vasily Kamensky's *His – My Biography of the Great Futurist* is an elaboration of pre-Revolutionary narratives about the duality of earthbound and celestial life as a defining feature of communist struggle.[11] An autobiography, it relates the heroic course of Kamensky's creative life as a parallel to the history of the communist struggle. In the introduction, Kamensky justifies his account by saying that literature, instead of dealing with fictional stories, must present the lives of inspirational, important, famous people, one of whom is the author himself. *His – My Biography* is conceived as a story about "the one and only Vasily Kamensky, the Great Poet, the

Winged Sage, the Futurist Poet-Warrior, Living Monument on the Mound of Creation."[12]

But Kamensky is not just a "living monument." In the biography two versions of the poet emerge: the earthly "I," a gluttonous, passionate, desiring man, and "him," the celestial angelic being. Kamensky explains the difference between his corporeal and incorporeal self: "He does not need anything […] I need everything. My greed is limitless: I want fame, money, comfort, health, love, wine, cigars, health resorts, doing things in a big way, drunkenness, youth, paintings, music, verse, circus, theatre, friends. I want everything that is around me."[13] He goes on to explore the duality in detail: "Him and me, me and him. Me – it is me when I eat a hearty and tasty meal, drink wine and black coffee, smoke a long cigar […] He is always in creative contemplation. He is incorporeal and light as an angel."[14]

This duality of the glutton and the angel, as a celestial version of the self, can be interpreted as a religious one – the duality of body and soul. But it is perhaps more appropriate to situate it in the context of a specifically Russian dialectic, originating, like cosmism, in the nineteenth century: the dialectic of *byt* and *bytie*.[15] These two notions are not directly translatable into English. *Byt* denotes ordinary, banal, everyday life, and *bytie* the enlightened, spiritual existence. In the mid-nineteenth century, Russian intellectuals developed an understanding according to which people can, by cultivating the spirit, liberate themselves from the shallowness, transience, and ugliness of *byt*. *Bytie* is the realm of the true, free self, and the task of the intellectual class is to lead the people toward it, toward political, intellectual, and artistic freedom, toward a secular non-place which replaces the life after death described by the Orthodox Church.

A good way to understand the interpretation of history specific to Russian futurism, and the revolutionary version of the evolving "will of the universe" that drives the past and future of humanity, is to look at the relationship between *byt* and *bytie*. This is a relationship between the time of earthly history – the here and now – and the transcendental state that history will reach at its end. In Kamensky's autobiography, this relationship is articulated as the camaraderie between the glutton and the angel. The angelic Kamensky, the creature of *bytie*, in the prose of 1918 does not lead a life above and beyond earthly existence. In the spirit of dialectical materialism,[16] so to speak, angelic spiritual existence depends on material life, on *byt*. The contemplative angel and the

Kamensky who likes to drink, smoke, and go to the circus are best friends. The ascent to *bytie* directly depends on Kamensky's efforts to transform and modernize *byt*: "He is tropical vegetation, and I am the Earth. His and mine, our life, is the flight of a bird with verse."[17]

The "flight of the bird with verse" is not only flight in a figurative sense. To launch the angel into the poetic ether, Kamensky has to learn to fly an aeroplane, to master modern technology. What stifles Kamensky is bourgeois *byt* in a provincial town. In the aftermath of the failure of the revolution of 1904, and his own failure to have his poetic genius recognized – the two failures presumably coincide – the futurist returns to his home town of Perm in the Ural region. In the company of his family and fellow citizens, he is divorced from his revolutionary and poetic ambition, which dampens his enthusiasm. Kamensky lives the life of a bored provincial scribe and his angelic double, the Poet, a life of despair. Kamensky writes about this situation:

The heart sank in permanent sadness.

Otherworldly creative thoughts and proud poetic forms [...] and the fervent fantasies about the advent of the futurist Word together with the vulgarity [*poshlost*] of the real: the talentless petite-bourgeois life [...] with managers and gossips, with relatives and inheritances, with idiocy and Perm newspapers, all that confused the Poet and bored Vassily, became monotonous, grew foggy in the fumes of petite-bourgeois philistinism.

And one wanted to work, create, live large.

[...]

He fell silent.

At first I got lost because of the increasingly abusive family cacophony and began being very irritated, dropping behind the Poet.

But soon I strengthened my will and began to strive for any kind of fulfilment.

Then Kamensky describes how he escaped the "fumes of petite-bourgeois philistinism":

The hour had come.

I decided to fly an airplane—farther.

The Poet immediately liked the idea.

What the flights of his searching Spirit missed was the flight of the body under the clouds, the swift discharge into the skies.

And I thought: The Poet will be my grateful passenger on the airplane and, most important, he and I will become the real futurists of our times, the Airborne Century.[18]

In this narrative about Kamensky's double self and the attempt to rise above the provincial *byt*, the Poet – that heroic and angelic self – lives with one wing in *bytie* and another in *byt*, the space of the everyday. His ascent, the path towards *bytie* at the end of history and the state of human perfection, depends on the transformation of the quotidian and the banal. This is the key difference not only between the notion of *bytie* in the nineteenth-century intellectual tradition and the communist one, but also between the Russian and the Western celestial utopias. Enthusiasm for things airborne is commonplace in Western avant-garde culture. The Italian futurists of the 1920s were obsessed with aeroplanes and invented aerial painting, "aviopittura," and aerial poetry, "aviopoesia."[19] In 1925, Le Corbusier presented his Plan Voisin from a bird's-eye perspective. Just as Russian leftist futurism differed from its fascist Italian version, however, Russian aerial imagination was different, not just politically but also aesthetically, in terms of the direction of the artistic and poetic gaze. The Russian futurists looked at aerial life forms not from above, but from their location within a life surrounded by merchants, relatives, philistinism, chaos, and desperation. Presentations of flying are created not from an authoritative, all-seeing, powerful position, but from the position of a subject deeply stuck in the mud of an unhappy *byt* – the frog's-eye perspective. Even when Kamensky calls himself "The Winged Sage" and "The Living Monument on the Mound of Creation," he is not a real hero, but a hero in becoming, partially an angel and partially a frustrated imperfect creature of the present – a hero-aspirant.

The perpetual coexistence of two protagonists of the Revolution, the transcendental (celestial) self and the immanent (earthly) self, defines the protagonist of communist utopia as a New Man in becoming, the same way socialism, in Soviet theory, is communism in becoming. This is why the final stage of history can be reached by technological means, through mastering the material environment. The camaraderie between Kamensky and Kamensky, the parallel evolution of "the will of the universe" and the quotidian, can be achieved by design.

The needs of the masses for mastery of space

The understanding that political change entails transforming the quotidian inspired the efforts of the architect Vladimir Tatlin. In 1917 Tatlin designed the Monument to the Third International, but during the course of the 1920s turned to the design of "new everyday life," devoting his attention to stoves, pots and pans, clothing, chairs. The final stage in his work was the design of portable, mass-produced wings, which he called the Letatlin.

In a photograph from 1932, the architect appears in the entrails of a wooden skeleton, modelled after a bird, which was later covered by canvas (Figure 1.3). Tatlin's huge nose replaces the bird's beak. The

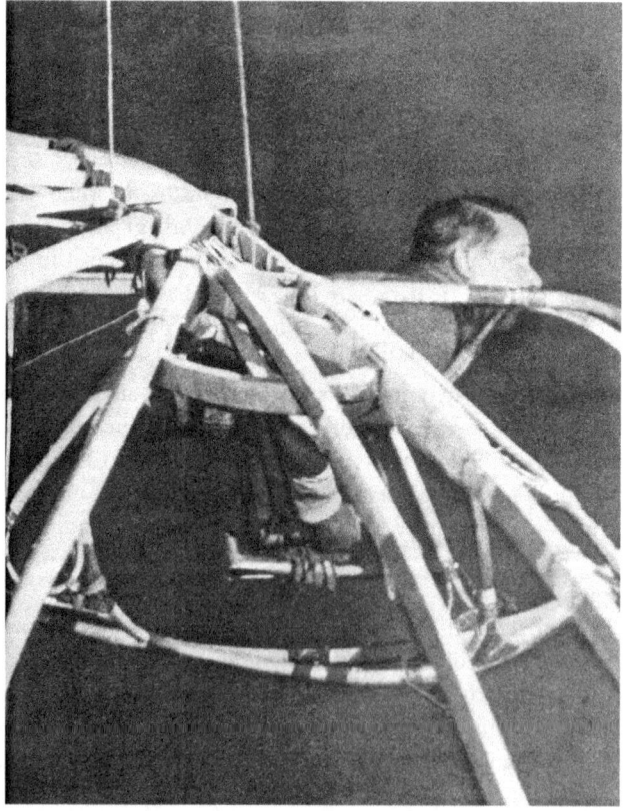

1.3 Unknown photographer. Photo of Vladimir Tatlin inside the Letatlin, 1932.

The will of the universe 23

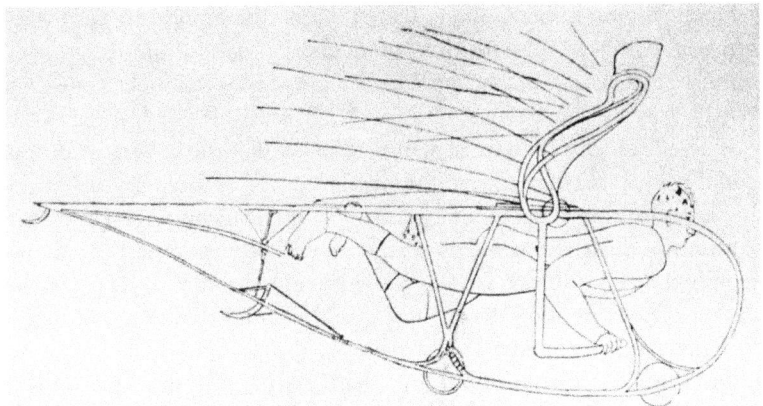

1.4 Vladimir Tatlin, Letatlin, drawing, 1932.

contraption was intended for everyday flying, and the flyer would operate the bird by flapping the wings with his arms and turning the pedals with his feet (Figure 1.4).

Tatlin considered the flying apparatus the culmination of his career:

> I proceeded from material constructions of the simplest forms to more complicated ones: these were clothes, objects of everyday life, up to the architectural construction in honor of the Komintern [Communist International]. The flying machine at the present stage of my work is the most complicated form that meets the needs of the moment for man's mastery of space.[20]

"*Letatlin*" literally means "flying Tatlin." It was intended to transform anyone using it into a winged creature, and thus improve everyday transportation. Tatlin's project would be mass produced, and ordinary citizens would use it for ordinary chores – going to work, for example. Building the Letatlin would launch the entire working class, in the spirit of communism, into the skies above Russia. The Letatlin was an angelic version of the architect and the ordinary Soviet man as the flying proletarian.

Tatlin's plan was that instruction in how to operate the wings would be introduced into schools, and would be as indispensable as learning how to swim, since it is actually akin to a kind of swimming. "A man in Letatlin will lie in the position of a swimmer," writes Tatlin, "and do the flying. He will work with his arms and legs as he already works when he is swimming. And that will be aerial swimming. For this swimming he will need to expend no more energy than for ordinary swimming."²¹ As he swims, the proletarian can enjoy themselves, making "small flapping movements" and "rocking in the air."²²

The author of the socialist wings believed that the advent of utopia could be facilitated by design – the design of *byt*, of the everyday world. In this transition the domestication of celestial technology is key, the creation of devices that the pupil, the housewife, the worker can use to master the realm of the skies as his alternative habitat. In this way the design of self (Letatlin, the flying Tatlin) becomes the design of a collectivity, of a class (a flying proletariat).

However, Letatlin and, with him, the Russian proletariat, did not end up ascending to celestial heights this way, since the design had technical problems. Tatlin consulted, according to his account, "specialists in the field of flying": a pilot and a surgeon.²³ He had based his calculations on the work of Otto Lilienthal, an inventor who worked on gliders, who in 1896 determined the ideal ratio between the surface of wings and the weight of the plane: 8 kilograms per square metre. Believing that he would eventually succeed, despite his lack of real expertise, Tatlin did not make one Letatlin, but three. Each version had a different weight and wingspan. Throughout the 1930s, the architect tried in vain to launch the wings in the fields on the outskirts of Moscow. The only time the Letatlin levitated above ground was in 1932, when it was hung from the ceiling at the Pushkin Museum of Fine Arts, next to Michelangelo's "David" (Figure 1.5). It had become art.

The failure of Tatlin's attempt to launch the proletarian into the skies could be seen to mean that the architect was driven not by an intention to improve proletarian life, to truly create a new *byt*, but rather by the pursuit of a perfect form, as some scholars have suggested.²⁴ This is not likely, however, because Tatlin apparent firmly believed that the Letatlin would fly, that he would be successful in his attempts to launch this architectural "form" so that it would enable the Soviet citizen to "master space." While the model hung in the Museum of Fine Arts, people gathered around Tatlin's pilots, and various versions of his wings, in suburban fields as featured in a photograph of Tatlin's launch attempt (Figure 1.6), in which the bare-chested observer seems to have acquired angelic wings.

The Letatlin was also not simply a formal experiment. It had the same function as Bogdanov's "red glasses," offering the opportunity to

The will of the universe

1.5 The *Letatlin* on display in the State Museum of Fine Arts, Moscow, in 1932.

1.6 Attempts to Launch Vladimir Tatlin's Letatlin, Moscow, 1933.

see, as a version of familiar everyday life, a new kind of lifestyle in which political and social evolution would be manifested. As such it had the potential to inspire a yearning for transformation. In Tatlin's interpretation, personal and social and evolution, as Tsiolkovsky would say, manifested the transcendental principle, the historical "will" hinged on repetition: the repetitive pursuit of a functional design, of a good calculation, of the event that would finally launch the proletariat into the skies.

"Stalin's falcons"

The celestial utopia originated in cosmism and evolved during the decades after the October Revolution into a series of visions of life in the sky, projects for facilitating the "mastery" of the skies as the last spatial frontier, and ideas about new revolutionary identities. The desire to master the skies and become a New Man was the result of revolutionary enthusiasm, the fervour for creating an evolved version of human existence. However, it was not only the enthusiasts who pursued these dreams. Myths of aeroplanes and celestial conquest were an important part of the government's promotion of the communist project. At the same time Tsiolkovsky, Bogdanov, Kamensky, and Tatlin developed exuberant visions of celestial conquest, the Soviet government mythologized flight as proof of socialist victory against the enemies of the Soviet Union. These narratives harnessed the pre-Revolutionary passion for aeroplanes and rockets and produced the official version of the winged New Man.

The government tradition of aerial fictions perhaps began with the formation of the "Red Fleet" at the end of the Civil War, in 1923. Although the state budget was depleted, the Communist Party decided to invest enormous sums of money into the development of aviation and the promotion of the newly founded Red Fleet. For eight months in 1923, articles on planes and pilots appeared almost daily on the front pages of the major newspaper, *Pravda*. These articles also invited readers to attend plane demonstrations and to join aero-clubs. Apart from nurturing and sharing the love of planes, the members of aero clubs throughout the 1920s also prepared for biological and aerial warfare and for defending socialism. Aeroplane-related myths and institutions were, for the Party, a way to create social cohesion and to establish the loyalty of Soviet subjects.

In the official Soviet aerial mythology of the next decade, the 1930s, the model of the socialist self appeared. Planes such as the "Ilya Muromets" were replaced by planes bearing the names of the great leaders of the Revolution. The early 1930s were the time of the Letatlin, the portable wings for the everyman. But they were also the time of megalomaniac projects, such as the Moscow–Volga Canal and the Moscow Metro, and, with them, the so-called "colossal aeroplanes." The first colossal aeroplane was designed in 1932 and named after writer Maxim Gorky. It was an "agit-plane," meant to spread the message of communism to the far reaches of the Soviet Union. It had a phone switchboard, a photo lab, radio transmitters, and a projector for screening propaganda films. Beneath its wings were lights for projecting text while the plane was in the air. The "Maxim Gorky" crashed in 1935, soon to be replaced by the "Vladimir Lenin," the "Joseph Stalin," and the "Maxim Gorky Two."

This curious situation in which planes become anthropomorphic – the mechanical doubles of great leaders – involved inventing a new version of the celestial self: "Stalin's falcon." Planes resembled people, but people could also resemble birds. "Falcons" were pilots of superhuman courage, determination, and strength, who celebrated the divine Stalin with their feats and were meant to be his sons. The most important of them was Valery Chkalov (Figure 1.7), who flew over the North Pole in 1937. He was described as "fearless in combat, but modest towards his friends … strict in work but affectionate towards children"[25] – the embodiment of an ideal communist. Chkalov fought for communism by conquering forces of nature: wind, rain, cyclones. In 1938, immediately after he died in a plane crash, 30 per cent of babies in his home village were named after him.

The "falcons" presumably defended the Soviet Union from all internal and external enemies. "Again and again you have shown the entire world that working sons of the socialist fatherland fly far, high and fast. They are terrified neither of the forces of nature nor of the base plots of the enemies of the people," said an article in *Pravda* in 1937.[26] But this was, in a way, a spiritual rather than a concrete defence. The development of the Red Fleet and the feats of the "falcons" were important as part of the communist mythology; they did not actually manage to defend the Soviet Union from its enemies. When Germans attacked the Soviet Union at the beginning of the Second World War, the Red Fleet was defeated in three weeks. Aeroplanes were celebrated in the media,

1.7 "Comrades Stalin, Chkalov, Kaganovich, Ordzhonikidze and Belyakov on the Shchelkovo Airport in 1936."

but they were not maintained in reality. The fleet was not a strong defence force in wartime, but it did serve the purpose of defending the myth of communism as the heroic land on the horizon and providing a template for the New Man.

Victors of outer space

In the 1960s, Tsiolkovsky's calculations were put to use and "falcons," the models of the victorious communist self, were replaced by cosmonauts, who competed with "capitalists" during the Cold War in attempting to be the first to conquer outer space in a "Space Race." Yuri Gagarin (Figure 1.8), Valentina Tereshkova, Aleksey Leonov, the members of the Vostok 1 crew, and others were each presented as a harbinger of progress, a being who "is not merely a victor of outer space, not merely a hero of science and technology, but first and fore most [...] a real, living, flesh-and-blood new man, who demonstrates in action all the invaluable qualities of the Soviet character, which Lenin's Party has been cultivating for decades."[27] They were smart, honourable, beautiful. While in reality they did not play a huge role in

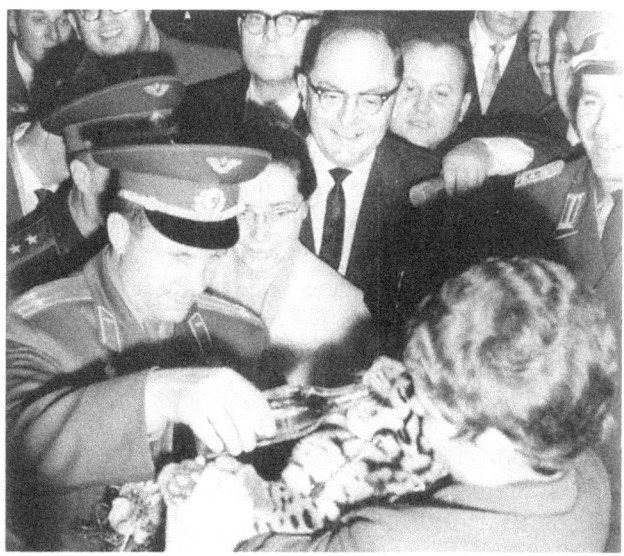

1.8 Yuri Gagarin and Valentina Tereshkova feeding a tiger baby in Berlin, 1963.

piloting the automated craft, they were celebrated as its brave pilots. They were chosen not for their piloting ability but for their talent for performance, since their main duty was to give speeches, on gruelling tours, about the victory of communism and their conquest of space across the Soviet Union and abroad. Their private lives were strictly controlled; they were not to appear unshaven, their clothing was always perfectly ironed, they always went to bed at the same time, and their spouses were often chosen for them.

In the realm below the cosmic heights, *byt* did not change much, nor was it perhaps meant to. Ordinary citizens, unlike the cosmonauts, had bickering wives and husbands, went around unwashed, got embroiled in fights, lived in cramped rooms, were burdened by poverty. Images from the Space Race were, for the ordinary citizen, images from a fantastic parallel world, a no-place above and beyond Soviet reality, somewhat like the mysterious realm beyond Soviet borders. The prominent critic and historian of Russian culture, Svetlana Boym, tells a joke from the time of the Cold War which goes as follows: "Armenian Radio asked the question: Why is it that the Soviet Union is not sending cosmonauts to the Moon? Answer: There is a fear that they will emigrate."[28]

The final launch

What actually happens when the Soviet citizen, immersed in celestial visions, emigrates? What happens when Soviet history, with its projections of victory over the skies, officially ends? The answer can be found in the fate of the last Soviet cosmonaut, conceived by the artist Ilya Kabakov in his installation "The Man Who Flew into Space from His Apartment" (Figure 1.9, 1.10). This work of the 1980s consists of a reconstruction of the melancholic interior of Soviet *byt*. The walls of a small room are completely pasted over with propaganda posters that celebrate the achievements of Soviet cosmonauts. Among them, the careful observer will notice, are calculations for a "do-it-yourself" version of a device for propelling the inhabitant into the skies. The device itself is there, too: a trampoline hung between the walls of the room. Beneath it is a wooden board supported by two old chairs, from which the citizen can climb the trampoline. On the floor is a pair of abandoned shoes. "The Man," it seems, succeeded in launching himself into the infinite space of the universe. The proof of his success is a hole in the ceiling.

The installation was initially presented in as part of a bigger installation called "Ten Characters," set up in the Ronald Feldman Gallery in New York in 1988, which earned Kabakov notoriety in the West. The larger installation is a reconstruction of a Soviet communal apartment – including a communal kitchen and communal toilet, hallway, and ten rooms – once inhabited by different "characters," such as "The Man Who Fled into his Painting," "The Man Who Collected Opinions of Others," "The Untalented Artist," "The Little Man," "The Collector," and the ultimate artist's alter ego, "The Man Who Describes His Life Through Other Characters." The inhabitants of these rooms, whose lives are explained in the narratives, are absent. But the site is populated by "little white people," white flies swarming in various parts of the installation, creepy angels replacing the missing inhabitants. The characters illustrate a variety of ways of dealing with the claustrophobia of everyday life, and modes of rising above it. The only thing that creates a "community," and any other kind of collectivity, is the physical space of the apartment; in a similar way, there is no clean and comprehensive image of the Soviet self, or of its metaphysical aspiration, beyond the exigencies of *byt*.

This need not be the end of the story. And it isn't. "The Man who Flew into Space from His Apartment" was assembled and disassembled

The will of the universe 31

1.9 Ilya Kabakov, "The Man who Flew into Space from His Apartment," Ronald Feldman Gallery, 1988.

several times, and in 2005–2006 it was presented in the Guggenheim Museum in New York as part of the exhibition of an exciting and exotic culture –"Russia!" – with an exclamation mark in the title. The installation was placed at the top of Frank Lloyd Wright's spiral, as the end and culmination of the history of Russian art. However, something peculiar happens here. The hole in the ceiling is not only an imaginary threshold between the domestic space of the ordinary Soviet citizen

1.10 Ilya Kabakov, "The Man who Flew into Space from His Apartment," exterior view.

and the celestial space conquered by cosmonauts. In physical terms, it is also the threshold between the Russian's reconstruction of his domestic space and the space of the global museum. There is one pair of shoes, but two missing men. One is the imaginary hero of Kabakov's story, and the other is the artist himself, who opened his habitat to the gaze of the Westerner and thus ceased to be a private person, launching himself into artistic stardom.

The Soviet cosmos has not disappeared; it has been displaced. The hole in the ceiling may have been intended to be the passage to Soviet utopia but, as staged, it is also the passage to global culture, embodied in the famous museum. "The Man" of the cosmonaut installation launched himself from the claustrophobic space of Russian *byt* at the end of Russia's history, but not into communism, the ideal classless society. This utopia has been replaced with another – with the utopia of a glamorous First World, of capitalism, which, from the perspective of the citizen of a former socialist country, seems akin to the skies of Soviet mythology.

Kabakov's installation captures one of the key features of celestial conquest as the paradigm of Soviet modernity. Technological zeal and aspiration, the main features of this discourse, reached their peak during the Cold War, and are a modernist commonplace. But in Russia they had an added dimension, because there was at the same time metaphysical zeal. Technology was effectively considered the means of transforming the mundane into the otherworldly. It was supposed to mediate the dynamic between *byt* and *bytie*, between the historical and the transcendental self. This approach was fundamentally materialistic. Architecture, which according to Tatlin is defined as the "means of the masses' mastery of space," facilitated ascent to the Soviet heavens, imagined as the ideal society at history's end. The transformation of the physical environment, of physical devices, of the quotidian, was supposed to produce the transfiguration of the Soviet citizen. Architecture in all these cases had a unique historical place, belonging both to *longue durée*, the time of everyday rituals and slowly changing social mores, and the heroic time of a turbulent political and social history. To master space was to link the quotidian life to the eternal, to link history to the idea of a perfect society at history's end. But it was also to link the quotidian to the heroic, to transform the commonplace and the quotidian so as to make the heroic possible. Technology of the material environment connected desperation to aspiration and the real to the imaginary, not only in the series of "celestial" voyages but also in the architecture of the home, the theatrical stage, the factory, the city. Case studies in the next five chapters examine this condition.

Notes

1 Asif A. Siddiqi, *The Red Rocket's Glare: Spaceflight and the Soviet Imagination, 1857–1957* (Cambridge: Cambridge University Press, 2010), 25–29.

2 Konstantin Tsiolkovsky, *The Will of the Universe: Unknown Intelligence; Mind and Passions*, trans. Svetlana I. Zherebtsova (Moscow: Pamiat, 1992) (*Volya vselennoi*, self-published in Kaluga, 1928).
3 Ibid., 5.
4 Ibid.
5 Ibid.
6 Ibid., 6.
7 Alexander Bogdanov, *Red Star*, trans. Charles Rougle (Bloomington: Indiana University Press, 1984), 60.
8 Tsiolkovsky, *Will of the Universe*, 6.
9 See Nikolai Krementsov, *A Martian Stranded on Earth: Alexander Bogdanov, Blood Transfusions, and Proletarian Science* (Chicago: Chicago University Press, 2011).
10 See Scott W. Palmer, *Dictatorship of the Air: Aviation Culture and the Fate of Modern Russia* (Cambridge: Cambridge University Press, 2006).
11 Vasily Kamensky, *Ego-moya biografiya velikogo futurista* (Moscow: Kitovras, 1918).
12 Ibid., 11; translation mine.
13 Ibid.
14 Ibid., 17.
15 Svetlana Boym, *Common Places: Mythologies of Everyday Life in Russia* (Cambridge: Harvard University Press, 1994).
16 The doctrine of dialectical materialism, based on the philosophy of Karl Marx – notably his *German Ideology* of 1846 – is an inversion of Hegel's dialectics. The development of ideas is based on the material conditions of production and, in the broader sense, the evolution of spirit depends on the evolution of matter. The term was introduced to the Russian-speaking world by Plekhanov and eventually became the basis of Marxism–Leninism.
17 Kamensky, *Ego-moya biografiya*, 11.
18 Ibid., 109.
19 An excellent article about *aeropoesia* is Willard Bohn's "Poetics of flight: Futurist aeropoesia," in *MLN*, 121, no. 1 (Italian Issue) (2006): 207–224. He observes that the majority of "aeropoets" had no flying experience, but relied on images of the Earth taken from an aeroplane and published in the popular press. This dominant mode of representation of airborne experience, rather than actual flight in the aeroplane, aided the construction of the "aerial view" representation of flight in avant-garde works.
20 Vladimir Tatlin, "Iskustvo v tekhniku!" (Art into technology) in *Vystavka rabot zasluzhennogo deyatelya iskusstv V. E. Tatlina* (Moskva-Leningrad: Gosudarstvennyi muzei izobrazitel'nykh iskusstv, 1932), 5–8, published in *Tatlin*, ed. Larissa Alekseevna Zhadova (New York: Rizzoli, 1989), 311.

21 From Isai Rakhtanov's essay, "Letatlin–an aerial bicycle," *Pioner* no. 9 (1932): 12, published in *Tatlin*, ed. Zhadova, 310.
22 From Zelinsky's interview "Letatlin," in *Vechernaya Moskva*, no. 80 (April 6, 1932) in *Tatlin*, ed. Zhadova, 30.
23 Tatlin, "Iskustvo," 311.
24 This is the thesis of Boris Groys in "Proizvedenie iskusstva kak nefunkcionalnaya mashina" (The Work of Art as a Non-functional Machine), *Proceedings of the International Conference: Vladimir Tatlin–Leben, Werk, Wirkung*, ed. Jürgen Harten (Koln: Du Mont, 1993). According to Groys, Tatlin's wings are art precisely because their author is a "technological dilettante." They are an attempt to achieve a perfect form, and not to create something that would actually function.
25 V. Kokkinaki, "Vdokhnovenny khudozhnik letnogo isskustva," *Literaturnaya Gazeta*, no. 70 (20 Dec., 1938): 30, cited in Jay Bergman, "Valerii Chkalov: The soviet pilot as a new Soviet man," *Journal of Contemporary History*, vol. 33, no. 1 (Jan. 1998): 140.
26 *Pravda*, 1937, cited in Bergman, "Valerii Chkalov", 139.
27 Evgeny Ryabchikov, "Volya; k pobede" (The will to victory), *Aviatsiya i kosmonavtika*, no. 4 (1962): 19, quoted in Slava Gerovitch, "'New Soviet Man' Inside Machine: Human Engineering, Spacecraft Design, and the Construction of Communism," in *The Self as a Project: Politics and the Human Sciences*, ed. Greg Eghigan, Andreas Killen, and Christine Leuenberger, *Osiris*, vol. 22, no. 1 (Chicago: University of Chicago Press), 135–157.
28 Svetlana Boym, "Kosmos: Rememberances of the Future," in Svetlana Boym (essay) and Adam Bartos (photographs), *Kosmos: A Portrait of the Russian Space Age* (New York: Princeton Architectural Press, 2001).

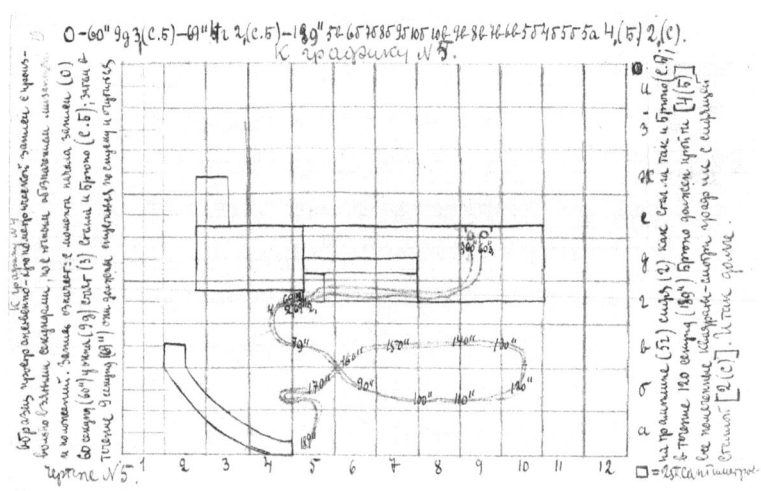

2.1 Vsevolod Meyerhold, plan of scenic movement for "The Magnanimous Cuckold," 1922.

2
Class unconsciousness

Meyerhold's chronotope

A scribble of ribbon winds over a grid (Figure 2.1). The axes are numbered, clearly intended to identify the spaces of the grid and thus to locate the ribbon precisely. The handwritten notes along the sides of the grid explain that the drawing is a "spatial-chronometric" notation of the scene – a plan of movement across the stage, with approximate timing. The drawing graphs the movement of two entities, marked "S" and "B," along with the time when they cross particular points. Although the author of this graph is obsessed with precision, describing the precise seconds of each moment of action, the overall result looks rather untidy. The trajectories of the moving objects are drawn freehand and the sloppiness of their outlines is in sharp contrast to the outlines of static objects on the grid.

The scribble on a grid is a plan of a scene in the play "The Magnanimous Cuckold," performed in Moscow in 1922 in the theatre of the director Vsevolod Meyerhold. The points on the stage, interpreted by Meyerhold in this drawing, coincide with "points of excitability," states through which an actor passes once he or she learns to perform scenic movement automatically, without conscious effort. This is the way in which the actors were supposed to present the farce, by the Belgian playwright Fernand Crommelynck, about an amorous misunderstanding between a miller, Bruno, and his wife, Stella. The play was transformed into the first ever "biomechanical" play, presenting a new kind of theatre for the socialist era. With the invention of a new theatre came the invention of both a new kind of space and a new kind of man, one who inhabits and traverses the new space and who understands movement and his own body in a way that corresponds to the demands of the modern age of technology and progress. The grid, as the typical modernist way to present and record space, defining an abstract, mathematical, infinite environment, is the embodiment of this age. The wiggly lines are an attempt to locate passion, love, desire in the modernist grid, to use the stage to present a new vision of space – a fusion of space and time, a chronotope.[1] The very lack of precision and neatness in what is intended to be a spatio-temporal blueprint for a precisely timed and choreographed performance indicates the complexity of modern theatrical space, a space for the performance of both precision and passion, both rationality and excitability. This space can, like the modernist grid, expand endlessly to cover the entire world, in the same way the Communist International was intended to spread over the entire globe.

Meyerhold's "biomechanical" proletarian actor performing in this space was trained to work in a chronotope, to think about his body and its actions as existing in both space and time, both in the real world and in non-place, the abstract space of the grid. What seems to be an eccentric scribble is, actually, a redesign of the common perception of space and the common perception of how the true proletarian was supposed to move, breathe, work, and live. It is meant to articulate proletarian identity and that proletarian *esprit de corps*, the excitement and blinding passions of group existence.

The world-machine

The idea of "biomechanics" and space coming together as a chronotope inhabited by a modern, progressive worker was actually created by a bureaucrat. Aleksey Gastev, the bureaucrat in question, was the founder of the Central Institute of Labour (*Tsentralny institut truda*, usually abbreviated to TsIT), an institution formed in the 1920s dedicated to training workers to develop precise, timed, efficient movements. Gastev was a member of the Social Democratic Party and a participant in the 1905 revolution, who spent some of the 1910s in Siberian exile and some working in Russian and European factories.

In pre-Revolutionary times, Gastev used verse to express his thoughts on communism and the workers' spirit. "The entire world will become a machine," he predicted, "in which the Cosmos will for the first time find its own heart, its own beat."[2] What moves the world and what makes the heart of the universe tick, according to Gastev's pre-Revolutionary vision, is the energy of the proletariat and its desire to join the great global machine moved by nothing but proletarian enthusiasm. Gastev's poetry celebrates the delirium of the masses caused by the encounter between the body and machine, an ecstatic state in which all drives turn into a collective urge to work; the force and the enthusiasm of the working people bring the machine to life:

> The crowd steps in a new march, their feet have caught the iron tempo.
>
> Hands are burning, they cannot stand idleness, they cannot be without a hammer, without work. Energy currents must be discharged.
>
> Strike, strike!
>
> Quicker! Faster!
>
> Chop, saw!
>
> To the machines!
>
> We are their lever, we are their breathing, their impulse.[3]

In this case, the proletariat is driven by a desire to merge with the collective body-machine in the fervour of labour. It is the desire for an orgasmic experience in which legs, arms, hearts, melt in delirium, and proletarian manic passion becomes the fuel of machine production. The fervour and desire of the working masses is cosmic desire, desire of man and the desire of the universe of "thousands of stoves-suns, atmospheres," of "Saturn's-fly-wheels."[4]

After the Revolution, Gastev developed his ideas in a series of articles published in *Pravda*. According to Gastev, that great collective desire of the working class – its machinic passion – should be the means of communist transformation, and to channel it properly is to start creating the new world. Describing his work as "rapture" and writing in a similarly raptured state, Gastev says,

> Force without quotation marks, real elementary, physical force.
>
> We have lived in hypocritical denial of force for too long.
>
> Force has to be the element of all social-cultural movements. It needs to be rehabilitated, worked upon, educated, encouraged. Let all masses learn to feel force, to breath force, to know its rough rapture.
>
> Force must create labour.[5]

To experience the rapture of "force," the worker has to first realize that his body is a machine like other machines. "Our first task," writes Gastev,

> consists of working with that magnificent machine that is so close to us – the human organism. This machine possesses sophisticated mechanics, including automatism and swift transmission. Should we not study it? The human organism has a motor, "gears," shock absorbers, sophisticated brakes, delicate regulators, even manometers.[6]

To become aware of his body as a machine, a machine that plugs into other machines such as those in the factory, the worker has to channel his "force." Irregular currents of desire have to be transformed into labour. "It is necessary," Gastev says, "to learn to govern one's body, to liquidate random physical dissoluteness, when the entire body does not work but helplessly wanders instead."[7] This is how a "breed of fine men, masters of main forms of movement" will come into being.

Gastev's "last work of art"

Gastev the poet in the 1920s turned into a government official, channelling his own passion into the project of engineering or "constructing" the ideal Soviet worker. From a poet who wrote about the delirium of labour and visions about the "mind of the universe," he became a state-sponsored bureaucrat and manager and approached the task of training the workers. In 1921, with Lenin's and Trotsky's support, he established the Central Institute of Labour. He considered this institution to be his "last work of art"[8] and the pinnacle of his poetic thought. It served to channel that vast "force" of the working class by imparting, in the journal *Proletkult*, "objectivity, normativity, and precision." He called this enterprise the science of "biomechanics."

Gastev founded his teaching on ideas developed at the turn of the century by the main proponents of improving labour efficiency, the Americans Frederick Winslow Taylor and Henry Ford.[9] He specifically adopted Taylor's principles of the "scientific organization of labour" (In Russian, *nauchnaya organizatsiya truda*, or NOT). He represented scientifically organized labour through "cyclograms." In Gastev's cyclogram, a photograph of workers is overlaid with a grid of movement that a particular labour operation involves (Figure 2.2). The result appears

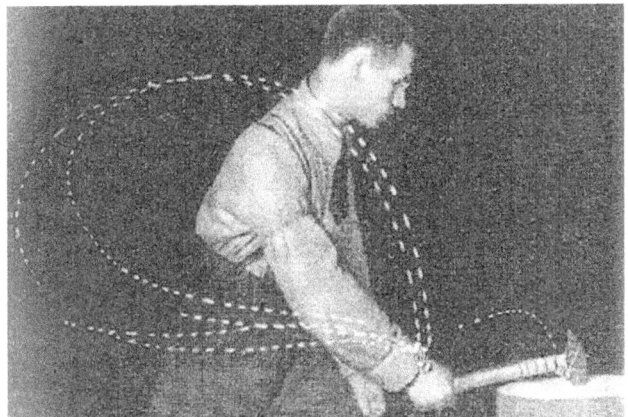

2.2 "Cyclogram of chopping wood with a chisel." Pedagogical Laboratory of the Central Institute of Labor, 1924.

quite similar to Meyerhold's plans for the stage. For Gastev, the graph denotes the "normal," most efficient way of performing a movement.

In his new institute, Gastev first examined chopping wood, demonstrated in Figure 2.2. After his passion for producing graphs of single operations was criticized for its myopic scope, he broadened his focus. He began to offer broader three- and six-month courses in work efficiency, intending to "create" the modern proletarian out of construction workers, textile workers, and aeroplane mechanics. He also founded three new disciplines that would contribute to this effort: "bioenergetics," "psychotechnics," and "social engineering." Had Gastev not been sent to the Gulag in 1938, the institute would have educated over a million workers.

Mass engineerism

Gastev's poetic ideas inspired, in new post-Revolutionary circumstances, not just a technology of organizing production, but also the design of a utopian vision of life and way of production for the future. Proletarian consciousness is precisely the consciousness of the machinic nature of the body, of society, of culture, of being – of the universe as a whole. The harnessing of the unstoppable, delirious yearning for labour and its transformation into (global) proletarian consciousness is what Gastev describes in his seminal work, "Proletarian culture is all in the future"

(Proletarskaya kultura vsya v budushchem), published in the journal *Proletkult* in 1919, during the Civil War.[10] The views developed in this article, to which his contemporaries responded with consternation – in the same issue Alexander Bogdanov challenged Gastev, calling him a "fetishist" and a "militarist"[11] – entailed a peculiar idea of "mechanized collectivism" of the international working class.[12] He attempts to provide a "molecular analysis"[13] of this topic.

As Gastev explains, the development of technology, with its "mechanization," "objectivity," "normativity," and "precision" of movement, created new sensibilities, a new "psychology" of the proletarian class.[14] Machines rule people to the same extent that people rule the machines. If machines are co-workers, they demand new kinds of movement, new kinds of thought, new kinds of feeling, and determine not only the nature of labour, but also the nature of society and culture. Since machine culture is the same across the world, Gastev says, the machines create an international proletariat that moves in a single rhythm, in a regulated and precise way. The identity of the international proletariat does not depend on politics or social mores, but on the involvement of masses in the processes of industrial production. The proletariat is "full of scepticism towards any kind of human feeling, and trust only in the apparatus, the instrument, in the machine."[15] The result is not only the mechanization of movement, but also the mechanization of thought. "No matter where it works," writes Gastev, "in Germany, in San Francisco, in Australia, or Siberia, [the proletariat] has only general psychological formulas, which are gaining their first outlines with the speed of an electric current, and which will culminate in a complex schematic system." The workers do not have personalities, they are anonymous, and turn into "proletarian units, such as A, B, C, or 325,075, etc." Instead of personality there are "powerful psychological streams, which flow from one part of the world to another, for which there are not millions of minds, but only one mind, that of the world." Instead of individual thought there is an "objective psychology," a kind of thought that resembles "psychological switching on, switching off, short circuits." Class consciousness is no longer the relationship of man to man but "the relationship of discrete groups of people toward discrete groups of machines."[16] In this relationship, the proletarian is a living force and a living machine. Their power lies in automatism, anonymity, in the negation of the soul, of feelings, and of all lyricism. Their consciousness is, according to Gastev's understanding, "mass engineerism."[17]

The missing proletariat

Gastev's entire theory of proletarian spirit fits in a peculiar and idiosyncratic way into the communist theoretical tradition. Karl Marx defined the notion of workers' "class consciousness" in *German Ideology* of 1885. It provided groundwork for communist thinking and introduced the notion that "ideology" is an inverted image of human life, in which material processes are the result of thoughts and ideas. According to him, the struggle to change the world and correct its injustices demands that revolutionaries "ascend from earth to heaven"; that they devote themselves to interpreting economic and material processes and the social relations stemming from them. "Consciousness," in Marx's terms, is in essence not a lofty and sublime intellectual pursuit, but the awareness of the "life-process," of social intercourse embedded in labour relations and processes. As he claims, "consciousness" is "conscious existence" in "actual life-process." Proletarian consciousness would be the awareness of the workers' role in the unjust social division of labour. As opposed to bourgeois theories according to which this division is natural, the conscious proletariat understands the division into mental and manual work, male and female roles, the rulers and the ruled, as historical and thus subject to change.

Lenin presented his interpretation of the Marxist agenda in *What is to be Done?* (1901). His theory was that it is the task of the intellectual vanguard (in this case, the Social Democrats) to instil political consciousness in the working class. According to him, the workers are capable only of spontaneous revolt and cannot grasp the big picture because of the powerful and omnipresent bourgeois ideology to which they are subjected and on which they cannot reflect. When Bolsheviks seized power some sixteen years after the publication of *What is to be Done?*, they set out to implement these ideas. However, they faced a peculiar problem. The working class, which was supposed to be liberated, barely existed.

The 3.5 million industrial workers living in Russia in 1917, Lewis Siegelbaum stresses, constituted only 2.5 per cent of the total inhabitants of the Russian Empire, far from the "majority of the oppressed" whose autonomy socialism paradoxically promised.[18] In the second half of 1920 the number dropped to 1.5 million.[19] The workers did not even form the majority of the urban population; in 1920, industrial workers constituted only 34 per cent of working adults in the cities. In addition, the majority of workers kept their ties to the countryside. During the Civil War, and throughout the 1920s, people migrated from country to city in search of food, from the city to the country in search of work, and also from the north to the south; the population was in complete transit. Everyone changed domiciles and professions. Aristocrats became bookkeepers. Red Army soldiers returned home to the countryside. Many children wandered the streets, homeless. In most cases, people employed in factories lived halfway between city and country, spending a considerable number of their working hours exchanging goods on the black market and, at harvest time, disappearing into the countryside to help their families.

The Communist Party had presumably freed the proletariat, and so the proletariat should support it. However, with few workers, and even fewer "class conscious" ones, the officials did not know who exactly its supporters were. The solution was to create a new, Soviet, proletariat. From the beginning of the 1920s, bureaucrats were obsessed with class analysis, classification, and statistics, trying to discover who the communist workers might be. There were endless attempts to separate the "working class" from the "bourgeoisie" and landowners, the so-called *kulaks*, and to trace people's pre-Revolutionary identities. The rituals of "unmasking" were introduced, in which people who wanted to pass as proletarians for opportunistic reasons were identified and condemned. Nevertheless, most people continued to claim that they belonged to the proletariat whenever it was convenient, to obtain housing or food, or to enrol in school.

The communist vanguard effectively had to create and define the Soviet proletariat before it started its work on "class consciousness." It was necessary to create the economic conditions for emergence of the proletariat by reforming the Russian economy. The political vanguard during the Civil War also took on the role of technological vanguard. In an effort to revive production during the Civil War and create a semblance of order, the Soviet government led by Lenin (paradoxically, albeit ambivalently) adopted American methods of production, such as Taylorism and Fordism. The methods that were essentially oppressing the American working class were supposed to be used to liberate the Russian working class. In this context, Western organization of production was not interpreted as capitalist, which is what it essentially was. It was rather, according to the Bolsheviks, military discipline necessary for the victory of communist forces. In fact, workers were now organized into "labour armies." Absentees were punished as "deserters." This militaristic spirit was coupled with a new notion of "class consciousness." Instead of leading the workers on the path towards spiritual enlightenment, the communist vanguard was reorganizing production, defining the proletariat in the process as a disciplined army. Through the process of production, workers were supposed to transform themselves into "class conscious" proletarians, a trope that became extremely prominent in heroic labour discourses of the Five-Year Plans in the 1930s era of centrally managed collectivization, industrialization, and consolidation of State power.

Gastev's belief that the collective proletarian spirit and the international unity of workers was a direct result of the modern processes of production belongs to this narrative and also reflects Marx's notion of "consciousness" being embedded into "life processes." His "scientific management" was part of the Bolshevik post-Revolutionary project of reforming production and "training" the working masses. But his notion of "consciousness" is peculiar in that it does not necessarily denote a conscious awareness of social and class relationships but a channelled desire, a passion for work, for machines, productive rapture, and ultimately the desire to create and become part of socialism as a cosmic apparatus. To train workers and create the proletariat was to use scientific management to cultivate and articulate natural passion and yearning, to join all working minds into one by creating "psychological switching on, switching off short circuits." What defines the culture of the New Man is not spiritual values, nor advances in "literacy and literature" – which are the pastime of "helpless," "contemplative" intellectuals – but rather a readiness to approach the entire world – culture, life, the environment – as a huge apparatus.[20]

Body-machine

The eccentricity and profundity of Gastev's notion of labour and "class consciousness" was echoed in its theatrical interpretation. To Gastev, the theorist of proletarian desire, labour did not simply mean work in the factory. To develop machinic class consciousness meant to conduct oneself as a machine in all realms of life, by becoming a body-machine. This meant practising biomechanics "in any room of the home, in the open air, in any workshop."[21] It is not labour "in the narrow sense of the word," but a sport, "such as sport in which movements are forceful, efficient, and at the same time light as air and mechanically artful."[22] The "biomechanics" of Gastev's framework is a science of everything that has to do with human embodiment, not just a science of movement but of diet, breathing, circulation, of "the special regime of behavior which is conducive to the correct circulation of matters in the organism."[23] In Gastev's vision, the proletarian goes around with various "instruments" packed in a "toilet case of culture" (*nesesser kultury*) and demonstrates the ability to "process, adapt, match one thing to another, add on, fit together, to masterly collect the scattered and the disorderly into mechanisms."[24]

Meyerhold was a great admirer of Gastev's "last work of art," the TsIT. Working after the Revolution with people who were not professional actors, he decided to train them in Gastev's manner, by adopting the "scientific organization of labour" as an aesthetic pursuit. He was not destined to train workers, but he could train actors; he could not improve factory production, but he could present it and perform it on stage. This performance, like Gastev's "scientific organization of labour," was an experiment in training the worker-machine and creating a collective consciousness that emerged from passionate and skilled factory work. In his lectures of the early 1930s, in which he reflected upon his work, he explained the first principle of biomechanics as the "body-machine, the worker – as a machinist."[25] The worker must be as efficient as a machine: "Extreme economy is needed in work, the utmost Taylorism. All tasks are fulfilled with minimal, most purposeful means."[26]

After the Revolution, Meyerhold worked with untrained actors, whom he intended to transform into a new proletariat of the stage. Meyerhold wanted, as Gastev did, to create a New Man – a theatrical one, trained for Taylorized theatrical production. For this purpose, the theatre director invented "biomechanical exercises," which grew in number during the 1920s. One of those exercises was called "Bow and Arrow" (Figure 2.3). In it, the actor pretends to draw back a bow and shoot an arrow, but he produces this effect only through movement, by contracting and releasing muscles, lifting and lowering his body. He was supposed to feel the presence of the invisible bow with his entire body and shoot the imaginary arrow in the most "efficient" way. In another exercise, called "Lowering the Weight," one actor lowers another actor, who stiffens his body in order to resemble an inanimate thing. In some exercises, such as "Slap in the Face" or a "Kick with a Foot," the actors would not actually touch each other. One actor "attacks" the other, who would pretend to be hit by an imaginary force. The most interesting exercises, however, were those in which the actors performed eroticized

2.3 "Bow and Arrow," biomechanical exercise.

actions, jumping or climbing one on another, swiftly and forcefully. In "Jump on the Chest," the actors could practise their sense of rhythm and their capacity to estimate distances. One actor would jump up onto another and curl his legs up onto his chest, and the other one would hold him while staring into his eyes. In "Jump on the Back" an actor would jump on the back of another actor, extending his hands out into the air to maintain balance.

Meyerhold's ideas about how the theatrical New Man was to be created resembled those of Gastev. People were to be trained, through a system of exercises, to move efficiently and become aware of their movement. Gymnastics, as a system of these exercises, was, for both Meyerhold and Gastev, something that Gastev described as "pure technique of movement, in which there could and could not be an everyday life necessity, but it is it, and only it which is the school of real training."[27] It "teaches the man to work" and its goal is to achieve the "bare automatism of labour."[28] But the differences are obvious. In Meyerhold's exercises there are no real machines or tools. In some cases the actor operates phantom machines. In others, he works with the bodies of other actors, climbing and jumping on them. The collective workers' spirit, the spirit of the proletarian actor, is expressed through abstract labour. Such labour no longer involves handling tools or apparatus, but rather operating only one's own body-machine, plugging one living mechanism into another, and also unplugging it.

Meyerhold similarly tried to establish a connection between coordinated factory work and scenic movement fit for the socialist age. But instead of merely mimicking production, his actors were to inspire it. Theatrical movement was supposed to be the most powerful and perfect instance of body management, and thus a model for the factory. It was in the theatre that proletarian enthusiasm – that "impulse" of the cosmic machine that Gastev writes about – was to be articulated. The "impulse" was to be directed and expressed by contracting and releasing muscles, stiffening and softening the organism, jumping, and synchronizing group movement. Theatre was not supposed to mimic labour; it was to reinvent it.

Class unconsciousness

The starting point for Meyerhold's "biomechanical" understanding of theatre and the performance of work was the rejection of the very notion of feeling. Gastev's "labour units" in the big global machine were to understand only "precise measurements, formulas, drawings, control calibers,"[29] without, as "sentimental philosophers" would have it, any feelings of "soul." The workers' drive is the same as the drive of the machine. There is only the relationship between "precise coefficients of excitements, mood, fatigue on one hand, and the graphs of economic stimuli on the other."[30] Meyerhold directly opposed Stanislavsky's method of psychological identification with characters and rejected psychology as the basis of theatrical performance, using an architectural metaphor:

> Psychology cannot provide a concrete solution for a number of reasons. Building the theatrical edifice on psychological foundations is the same as building a house on sand: it will inevitably be torn down by those who pay attention to physical states [...] All psychological states are conditioned by certain physical processes. As he finds the correct form of his physical state, the actor assumes the position in which a certain "excitability" arises in him, which takes over the audience, drawing them into the actor's art (this is what we earlier called "capture"), and this is the essence of acting. An entire range of physical positions and states is at the foundation of those "points of excitability," which colour themselves with this or that feeling.
>
> The foundation of this system of acting, of "arousing feelings," is always: physical foundation.[31]

The audience is drawn into the performance not because it identifies or establishes a psychological rapport with the protagonists, but because it reaches "excitability" together with the actors. The theatre communicates in a raw, visceral way. In this theatrical edifice, space is imagined as a system determined by the positions of the body and "points of excitability." Space is not to be comprehended rationally, but by forming a picture of the stage on the basis of bodily sensations. The most important task of the actor is "the cognition of self in space," which is only possible when one "knows one's own body so that, assuming one position or the other, one can precisely know what it looks like in a given moment."[32]

The actor who "knows" his body, however, is not consciously aware of his movement. That internal picture of the body comes from automatic action and reaction. In short, a spatially educated actor is an unconscious actor. He is not a rational and reflexive individual, but a creature of reflexes. A creature completely guided by the convulsion of his muscles and limbs. Meyerhold divides acting into three "moments": "The intentional moment, the realization of intention in reflexes, voice, movement, and 'reaction' – the moment in which all movements become reflexes and the cognitive aspect is reduced to a minimum."[33] Reflexes are turned into "excitations," "excitations" turn into a biomechanical spatiality, which is, in essence, a scheme of "points of excitement" and transitions from one point to another.

Life, organized

This performance at the limits of consciousness was supposed to provide a model for moving, feeling, experiencing everyday life. Boris Arvatov, the prominent theatre critic, comments on this in his account of biomechanical theatre "From theatre directing towards a montage of everyday life." According to him, the true power of theatre was the power to create a virtual *byt* – everyday life, intensified and reorganized, more comprehensible and more real. He starts his piece with a lament on alienation, chaos, and powerlessness in the post-Revolutionary world of possessions, feelings and action:

> We live in a disharmonious universe of mechanically produced things, which we do not feel; of feelings we do not believe in; of movements which we are not capable of directing. We do not govern *byt*, it governs us instead – governs with its spontaneity and lack of organization. And we wallow in it like frogs in mud and croak like frogs when it rains.

[...]But that is why we have theatre. There people teach and speak and lie and go for visits. There they make things and organize forms. There we have organized *byt*.

Organized how?

Aesthetically![34]

To organize *byt* aesthetically, in Meyerhold's case, was to establish a dialogue with Gastev and to use theatre to make everyday life resemble production in its gracefulness, efficiency, and "aesthetics." What makes the theatre of everyday life different from the theatre of illusion, according to Arvatov's "Theatre as production" (Teatr kak proizvodstvo), is the application of Taylorization, psycho-technics, and the rational study of movement. Instead of reflecting life, Taylorized theatre has transformative power, is "life-creating theatre" (*teatr zhiznetvorchestva*).[35]

The power of theatre to create new modes of life rests on its ability to produce new embodied subjects – new ways of moving, seeing, and operating the environment. It is not that it represents work in the factory, but it is, as Arvatov wrote, "the factory of a qualified man."[36] To qualify the public was to immerse it in this virtual everyday of mechanical existence – *byt* brought to the level of higher intensity, transformed, and created anew.

House as a machine for playing

The spatiality of this theatrical world is represented in the image discussed at the beginning of this chapter (Figure 2.1) – the recording of a scene in "The Magnanimous Cuckold," a theatrical, transformed version of everyday life. The plot is rather banal. A village scribe and miller, Bruno, is so jealous of his wife, Stella, that he forces her to make love to all the men in his village so that he can discover who her "real" lover is. The village descends into chaos, and jealous women chase Stella. In the end she leaves with one of her partners. Meyerhold succeeds in transforming this romantic farce into a presentation of proletarian "force," an expression of the spirit of efficient factory work, as a model for everyday existence. In his interpretation, the passion of a lover becomes the eroticism of collective ardour. The play functioned both as a comedy and a vision of proletarian life in becoming.

This attempt to perform Crommelynck's plot and at the same time to demonstrate the principles of "biomechanics" as a model for contemporary proletarian life was realized on a non-perspectival stage. The stage of Meyerhold's theatre was, as a contemporary would describe it in 1924, "entirely naked": "Everything was taken down, and the immense empty space of the theatre scene produced a dark impression. What was especially overwhelming was the dirty damp brick wall, the only background of the spectacle."[37] This approach corresponded to Meyerhold's stance that theatre is not representation, not an "image" of life or of visual phenomena. Instead, it is a performance of life. It is the creation of excitement, a form of visceral communication. According to Meyerhold, there are no projections on the stage, but real people, "phenomena in movement." Meyerhold wrote, "A living picture – does it not seem artistically absurd? […] There is no reason a picture would be alive. Something alive should not be a picture, living things should be in a state of movement."[38] Theatrical "biomechanics," like those of Gastev, are a "contemporary science" of turning "haphazard" movement on stage into a system.[39]

Movement, life, passion: all are kinds of production. But Meyerhold's production was theatrical and it took place in a theatrical machine (Figures 2.4, 2.5). This machine, designed by Lyubov Popova – an important protagonist of the 1920s Russian avant-garde – followed the movements of actors. They jumped on it, turned it, crawled along it, and danced on it in the spirit of the "biomechanical" worker who attaches to a machine and breathes life into it. It consisted of two platforms, two ramps, two staircases, three wheels, scaffolding, and a revolving door. In front of the machine there was a tilted curved bench.

Bruno's mill was reduced to the basic elements of floors, doors, walls, and wheels, recombined into theatrical machinery. Instead of representing a particular kind of production machinery, the transformed house was a universal machine, the same way that Meyerhold's scenic movement was a performance of universal labour – labour as a principle of movement. As a universal machine, and depending on how the actors operated it, the set's function could change throughout the performance, from a room into a morning terrace, from a terrace into a dining room, from a dining room into a courtyard.[40] The wheels and the windmill turned in accordance to the psychophysical state of the actors. For example, when Bruno was in the throes of his jealousy, the wheels would start to rotate fast, stopping when he calmed down.

2.4 "The Magnanimous Cuckold," poster with set design by Lyubov Popova, 1922.

2.5 "The Magnanimous Cuckold," set design by Lyubov Popova for the 1928 performance.

"A premeditated attempt to murder theatre"

The actors' movements were at the same time comical and delirious, efficient and excessive. Alma Law has reconstructed the performance based on the recollections of contemporaries.[41] She describes how in the first act the actors start to "operate" the revolving door. One actor, playing the Major, bows and then hits the door with his behind, hitting another actor, Petrus, who flies into the air and falls on the bench, hitting the third actor, Estriug, who is sitting on it. Then the Major leans on the right half of a revolving door, the door turns and the left half hits him in the nose. Holding his nose, he passes through the door. A fourth actor, Bruno, passes through the door behind him, and the two go in circles through the door. The scene aroused "excitation" – in this case, laughter –in the audience precisely because it worked as a fast mechanism, in which the actions of performers triggered one another automatically, setting in motion, at the same time, the scenic house-machine.

This entire scene resembles slapstick comedy in silent film. And it is not a coincidence. In fact, Meyerhold writes about the cinematographic style of Charlie Chaplin in a speech of 1929, "The new battle on the theatrical front" (Novy boy na teatralnom fronte).[42] The director explains, in a similar fashion to Gastev, that the language of movement connects the proletariat around the world and that the global masses belong to a universal culture of movement. That culture of movement is created not only through factory work but also through performance and film. "Charlie Chaplin," Meyerhold writes,

> is extraordinary inasmuch as he does not speak. If we are to understand him as our own, as an actor speaking his language in any country, he has to remain silent. Then in Japan, in Moscow, in China, in India, in the North Pole, in the land of Samoyeds and elsewhere, he appears familiar […] If Charlie Chaplin now began to talk in English, Soviet peasants would not understand it. The peasants would say: a "beautiful" actor, but why does he babble? And when he starts babbling in a language unknown to them, they won't accept the film.[43]

"The Magnanimous Cuckold" of Meyerhold's staging is an interpretation of drama in a language of scenic movement that connects the masses of the world: the proletariat in becoming. The costumes were designed to allow for maximum expressivity of movement, but also to establish a relationship between the world of the play and the world of production. The production clothing, the so-called *prozodezhda*

2.6 Lyubov Popova, costume for "The Magnanimous Cuckold," 1922.

(Figure 2.6), also designed by Lyubov Popova, was intended to resemble workers' uniforms, to manifest the idea that theatre is a genre of production. Both men and women wore large shirts, and the men also wore loose pants and the women short skirts. Only props differentiated dramatic roles: pom poms, an apron, a hat.

One critic disliked the machinic nature of the play's choreography and set design and noted a difference between the logic of Meyerhold's theatre and constructivism: "The model of L. Popova is unsuccessful not because of its constructivism, but because of its machinism," he writes.[44]

Almost confused with production, taking machines, mechanics, instead of the constructive model, they took the machinic model, which has no connection with real action. Here we do not have accident, but something much worse – a premeditated attempt to murder theatre. This premeditation is testified to by the *prozodezhda*, which does not have even a small relation to the theatre in its make and colour.[45]

What the critic failed to appreciate was the director's and set designer's intent. The *prozodezhda* was to help define theatre as a collective, anonymous endeavour, rather than an ensemble of individual actors with individual psychologies. Instead of commotions of the soul, a collective trance of a bodily apparatus works together with Popova's set apparatus. The performance of "The Magnanimous Cuckold" depended on a collective mechanics – a precise, efficient mechanics of a body in delirium. This mechanics is at times the mechanics of general disarray, at times the synchronized movement of a well-oiled collective machine. In the third act, for example, the "suitors" wait for their turn to sleep with Stella. As they chase another character, the Cowhand, across the entire stage, they perform acrobatic tricks – jumps, handstands, spins – and the windmill turns in different directions with the rhythm of action. When Stella announces that whoever leaves will lose his place in the queue, the "suitors" cry, "All in line!" and start dancing *chechotka* (a traditional Russian folk dance) (Figure 2.7). The mechanics of disarray,

2.7 *Chechotka*, in "The Magnanimous Cuckold" rehearsal of 1928.

in which one actor reacts to the acrobatic movements of the other, form a rhythm of collective movement that interrupts the plot in order to present this transformation of actors' bodies into one body moving in a manic rhythm.

Sketches, encore

When Meyerhold "murdered" theatre, as the critic put it, he "murdered" the perspectival set, but he also created a new kind of space, the space of collective rapture. The sketches for the stage world of the "Magnanimous Cuckold," such as Figure 2.1 discussed at the beginning of this chapter, are invaluable for understanding Meyerhold's spatial imagination. Rather than a space stabilized by the perspectival image, this was a space of "excitations," of mental and physical states created by and intersecting with machine and man.

Another drawing of scenic movement (Figure 2.8), created by Meyerhold, is, the handwriting explains, "an approximate recording of the first scene in the first act." It depicts the action of four characters, Stella, Cornelius, Florance, and Nurse, as the text above the grid says. The image is similar to that discussed at the beginning of this chapter and belongs to the same series. It is also a series of meandering lines superimposed over the outlines of Popova's set. But here there is no grid.

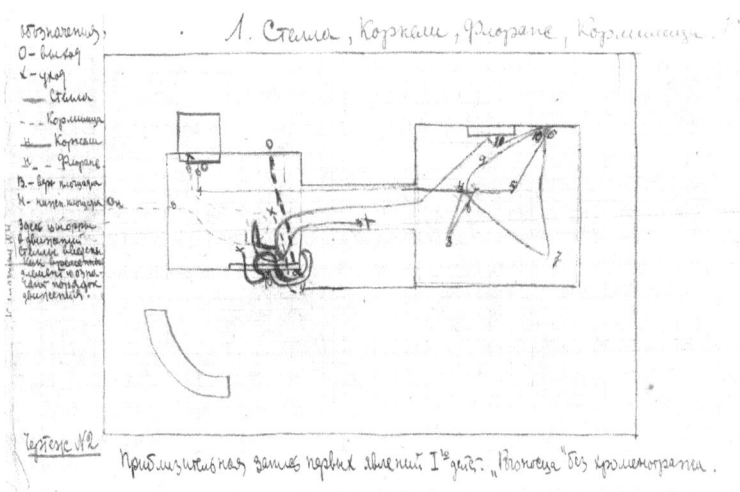

2.8 Vsevolod Meyerhold, "Stella, Bruno, Florance, Wet Nurse" (plan of movement for the "Magnanimous Cuckold"), 1922.

The lines connect specific points on the set – a cross and a circle – and tangle together at one end of the construction in a complicated knot. On the margins of the drawing, Meyerhold writes that the lines represent the movement of characters across the stage, between the "entrance" (cross) and "exit" (circle).

The drawing is a recording of the actor's Taylorized "labour" and a scientifically organized production of "excitations." An "excitation" occurs between entry and exit, and is here plotted onto a grid. This is not entry into and exit from physical space but the path, carefully choreographed, into and out of group delirium. The group action comes together on the grid as a barely intelligible scribble, a knot at the edge of the construction. Proletarian actors in the state of unconsciousness, performing theatrical work in an automatic way, wrap their bodies around each other and wrap the body-machine around the architectural machine, performing chaos.

Meyerhold's drawings are an effort to describe this chaos, to record it and control it; they are plans for an architecture of delirium. Meyerhold's "plan," though perplexing, and looking quite unlike Gastev's perfectly regular cyclograms, is nevertheless not a complete travesty of Gastev's ideas about the image of regulated movement. This is also an industrial space in which "proletarian units" of a completely mechanized world connect, switch on and off, experience "short circuits" of class consciousness.

Meyerhold's architecture for theatrical production is a spatio-temporal architecture, based on his principle that "theatre is an art which (unlike other arts) happens both in time and space," whose "turnaround performed in physico-mathematics will produce new conditions in the theatre."[46] The time-space introduced by "physico-mathematics" is presented in a drawing that features a scene with three actors, Stella, Bruno, and Nurse (Figure 2.9). This drawing is peculiar in that it separates stage action from physical space. The set of connected rectangles, repeated in every drawing, appears, but here the meandering curves connecting crosses to circles move across the outlines of the stage structure, as if it didn't exist. Only two points are anchored once to the edge of the platform. All other trajectories seem to be situated in an aerial space above and beyond the stage, a space in which smooth and completely continuous movement is possible. The result seems to be an architecture that no longer relates to either any concrete tools of production or to the fixed scenographic machine.

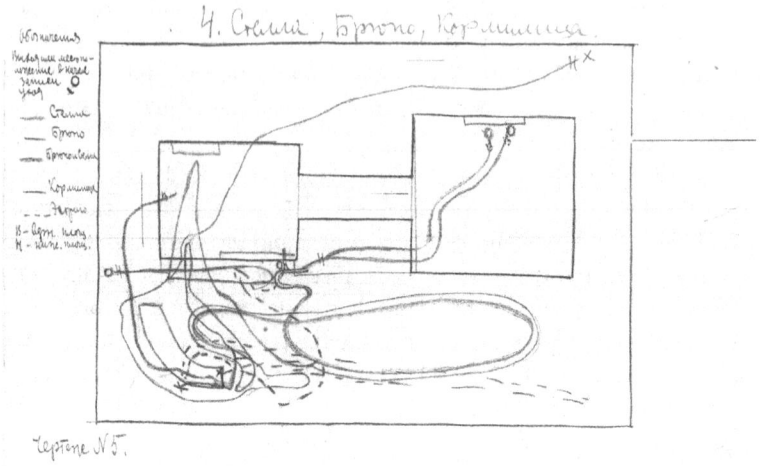

2.9 Vsevolod Meyerhold, "Stella, Bruno, Nurse" (plan of movement for the "Magnanimous Cuckold"), 1922.

Space of excess?

Meyerhold's biomechanics need not be seen as a bad translation of the principles of Gastev's "scientific organization of labour." His system employed the same means of representation and utilized the same concepts. It was a vision of what can happen when these principles are brought to their final conclusion, when they are pushed to their limits and the space inhabited by the electrified, delirious proletariat, like the one Gastev described in "Proletarian culture is all in the future." In a country in which proletarians were few – but where their liberation justified the entire political system – the world-machine and the transformation of the populace into a collective proletarian body were utopian endeavours. Meyerhold, unlike Gastev, articulated the space of this utopia as the theatrical world-machine. This was a space in which proletarian consciousness became proletarian unconsciousness, as Taylorized movement became frantic and automatic, and the performance drove both the actors and the audience to delirium.

The combination of (supposedly) Taylorized movement with a story about sex, passion, and jealousy added a completely new dimension to the notion of "biomechanics" and to the "scientific organization of labour." It eroticized the science of labour, building on Gastev's idea of labour as something utterly carnal – an expression of proletarian ardour and the passions of production. This did not escape his contemporaries, some of whom were shocked by the "lewdness" of the entire performance. Here is what one theatre critic writes:

> When you look at all these wheels, scaffolding, spring-boards, cages, turning doors, windmills, and such scenic devices among which our young actors yell, somersault, jump on top of each other, dance Hottentot dances like animals, performing sadistic, pornographic tasks of foreign and domestic morphinists and charlatans, one barely refrains from screaming; this is the utmost mockery.
>
> And what is only done inside those studios in all these kinds of laboratories of the young actors. What a vacant soul, what an unscrupulous depraved existence, what sorry apes and acrobats of the body and soul must be produced by these studios where young people engage in "biomechanics," whose image we have seen last night in the state theatre: jumping on top of each other, dragging each other like animals […] and speaking, with the innocence of saints, the most vulgar and obscene things.[47]

That fantastic "pornography" was, in fact, the raw, naked presentation of principles developed from a bureaucratic notion of the 1920s about constructing the proletarian class. It was in the theatre, the double of the Russian factory, that the proletarian – that elusive being the government was supposed to identify, classify, train, and shape – was created. It turned out that this proletariat – or Meyerhold's, at least – was obscene rather than decent. The excess energy, to be channelled by the "scientific organization of labour" promoted by the Soviet State and used in industrial production, is excessive in another respect: because it is erotic, passionate, and, in a wonderful way, ugly. As is the New Man it produced.

In effect, Meyerhold manages to foreground the "perversity" of Gastev's interpretations of labour, proletarian consciousness, and the programme for Soviet technological and ideological progress. This perversity consists in the notion that the moulding of the proletariat is the moulding of affect; that work training is the channelling of enthusiasm; that proletarian consciousness is love, desire, passion, rather than self-awareness. Gastev's theories and "training" methods were part of the Soviet master narrative, discussed in the previous chapter, in which technological zeal figures as metaphysical zeal, the yearning for transcendence. A strange participant in this discourse, Gastev established that the ultimate goal of communism is to synchronize workers' "impulses" with those of the cosmos, which, like the body, is a delirious machine. Meyerhold translates this into theatre by creating a time-space of abstract labour, which is the time-space of a sensual, even lascivious, interaction of embodied machines. By using biomechanics as a theatrical strategy in a performance about sexuality, Meyerhold presents and enacts two radical notions. The first is that proletarian class consciousness is, at its foundation, erotic. The second is that the yearning for transcendence, often implicit in socialist programmes, and explicit in Gastev's proposals for the future of the working class, is a sexual yearning.

Versions of this radical philosophical stance reappear later, and without direct connection to Meyerhold, in leftist interpretations of psychoanalysis, such as that of Wilhelm Reich or Gilles Deleuze and Félix Guattari. The uniqueness of this first eroticization of labour and politics, however, is that it did not stem from psychoanalytic teaching but was a radical and non-ironic version of the communist economic and political programme. As such it is a perfect demonstration that narratives about embodiment were actually historically linked to narratives about communism. And, more importantly, that architecture – the project of translating ideas into a spatial logic, of mapping the practice of workers' liberation – revealed this erotic dimension of the communist project as it literally "fleshed out" narratives about progress, technology, and class identity.

Like Western texts based on similar premises, such as Deleuze and Guattari's "schizoanalysis"[48] or Reich's treatises on sexual liberation,[49] biomechanical architecture is more potent in its artfulness, in its *poiesis*, than in the neatness and "rationality" of its polemic. That, however, might perfectly reflect its main purpose – to present leftist politics as a practice driven by passion, yearning, and zeal. In the Soviet context, biomechanics is a uniquely radical and eccentric interpretation of communism and its ideals. But the tendency to relate the political to the intimate, to turn ideas about labour into ideas about the material environment, figured prominently in Soviet architectural narratives of the 1920s and the 1930s. In the next chapter I will discuss another, quite different, aspect of this approach to the space of labour. It is the logic manifested in objects which constituted what Peter Sloterdijk imaginatively called the "self-container," the individual architectural envelope.[50]

It figured as a site of "rationalized" rather than dramatized life, an instrument of a different kind of discipline.

Notes

1 The term "chronotope" is originally a Russian term – *khronotop* – created by combining Greek terms for time and space. Its most prominent theoretical use is that of Mikhail Bakhtin, who used it to describe the key characteristic of a literary text – a specific configuration of the time and space presented within it. (For more, see Mikhail Bakhtin, "Forms of Time and the Chronotope in the Novel," in *The Dialogic Imagination*, trans. Caryl Emerson and Michael Holquist (Houston: University of Texas Press, 1981), 84–258.) This term was introduced into the theory of architecture (at the heyday of its close engagement with literary theory) by Michael Hays, in his edited volume, *Hejduk's Chronotope* (Princeton: Princeton Architectural Press, 1996). In it, the opus of New York architect John Hejduk is examined as a combination of writing and design, story and image, that is, time and space. A theatrical performance can be understood as a chronotope, as a spatialization of a written text, in this sense. This is especially appropriate in the case of Meyerhold, who conceptualizes and represents his work with "spatio-hronometric" recordings. Here, the chronotope is captured as an image. This practice stems from the culture of calculating and presenting efficient movement in the context of labour-saving and management practices, such as those discussed on the pages that follow.
2 Aleksei Gastev, "My Posyagnuli" (We encroached), in *Poeziya Rabochego udara* (Petrograd: Izdanie Proletkulta, 1918), trans. Kurt Johansson in Kurt Johansson, *Aleksej Gastev: Proletarian Bard of the Machine Age* (Stockholm: Almqvist & Wiksell International, 1983), 131.
3 Ibid., 76.
4 Ibid., 131.
5 Ibid., 59.
6 "Trenazh" (Training), *Pravda* (16 Nov. 1922), republished in Aleksey Gastev, *Kak nado rabotat: prakticheskoe vvedenie v nauku organizatsii truda*, eds N. M. Bakhrakh, Y. A. Gastev, A. G. Loseva, E. A. Petrova (Moscow: "Ekonomika," 1966), 51; emphasis mine.
7 Ibid.
8 Editors, "Aleksey Kapitonovich Gastev i ego 'poslednee khudozhestvennoe proizvedenie'" (Aleksey Kapitonovich Gastev and his "last work of art") in Gastev, *Kak nado rabotat*, 6.
9 In the 1880s and the 1890s, Frederick Winslow Taylor developed the notion of the "scientific organisation of labour," which involved applying engineering principles to managing labour processes. He would analyse

labour in terms of workflows and attempt to make these workflows more efficient. In pursuit of efficiency, he developed motion studies and analysed workers' motivation. Henry Ford, the automobile manufacturer, did not build on Taylorism directly, but he also worked, in the 1910s and the 1920s, on increasing efficiency by standardizing products and by applying the principles of the assembly line to make production faster and cheaper.

10 Aleksey Gastev, "O tendentsiyah proletarskoy kulturi: Proletarskaya kultura vsya v budushchem" (On the tendencies in proletarian culture: Proletarian culture is all in the future), *Proletarskaya Kultura*, nos. 9–10 (1919): 35–45.
11 Alexander Bogdanov, "O tendentsiyah proletarskoi kulturi (Otvet A. Gastevu)" (On the tendencies in proletarian culture (A response to A. Gastev)), *Proletarskaia Kultura*, nos. 9–10 (1919): 46–52.
12 Gastev, *Proletarskaya kultura*, 44.
13 Ibid., 36.
14 Ibid., 42.
15 Ibid., 44.
16 Ibid., 44.
17 Ibid., 45.
18 Lewis H. Siegelbaum, *Soviet State and Society between Revolutions, 1918–1929* (Cambridge: Cambridge University Press, 1992), 26.
19 Ibid., 27.
20 Aleksey Gastev, "Snarzhaites, montery!" (Get ready, fitters), *Poeziya rabochego udara*, 205–206.
21 Gastev, "Trenazh" (Training), *Pravda* (16 Nov., 1922), republished in *Kak nado rabotat*, 51; emphasis mine.
22 Ibid.
23 Ibid., 52.
24 Ibid.
25 Meyerhold, "Principles of Biomechanics," in a compilation of lectures written by students of GVTYM (Gosudarstvennye Vyshie Teatral'nie Masterskie – State Higher Theatre Workshops) compiled by Korozhov, RGALI, Fond 998, Opis 1, Document 740, 42.
26 Ibid.
27 Gastev, "Trenazh," 53.
28 Ibid.
29 Gatsev, "Nashi zadachi" (Our tasks) (Moscow: Institut truda, 1920), republished in Gastev, *Kak nado rabotat*, 26.
30 Ibid.
31 Meyerhold, "Akter budushchego" (Actor of the Future) presentation in the Little Hall of the Conservatory, 12 May 1922, in RGALI, Fond 998, Opis 1, 740, 4.

32 Lectures in set design and biomechanics read in the first year of GVTYM in the school year 1921/1922, RGALI, Fond 998, Opis1, 738, 5.
33 Meyerhold, "Principles of Biomechanics," 42.
34 Boris Arvatov, "Ot rezhissury teatra k montazhu byta," (From theatre directing towards a montage of everyday life), in *Ob agit i proz isskustve* (*On Agitation and Production Art*) (Moscow: Izdatelstvo "Federatsiya," 1930); originally in *Zrelishcha*, no. 24 (1923).
35 Boris Arvatov, "Teatr kak proizvodstvo," (Theatre as production), in *Ob agit i proz isskustve*, 138; originally in *Gorn*, 1, no. 6 (1922).
36 Ibid., 132.
37 Nadezhda Vladimirovna Gilarovskaia, *Teatralno-dekoratsionnoe iskusstvo za 5 let* (*Theatre-decoration Art in the Last 5 Years*) (Kazan: Kombinat Izdatelstva i pechati, 1924), 24–25.
38 Vsevolod Meyerhold, *Lektsii 1918–1919: Instruktorskie kursy, kursy masterstva stsenicheskikh postanovok, shkola akterskogo masterstva* (*Courses for Instructors, Courses in the Art of Set Design, a School of Actor's Art*) (Moscow: O.G.I., 2001), 25.
39 Ibid.
40 Boris Alpers, *Teatr sotsialnoi maski* (*Theatre of the Social Mask*) (Moscow: Gos. izd-vo khudozhestvennoi literatury, 1931), 3.
41 Alma H. Law, "Meyerhold's 'The Magnanimous Cuckold,'" *The Drama Review* [TDR] 26, no. 1, Historical Performance Issue (Spring, 1982): 61–86.
42 Vsevolod Meyerhold, "Novy boi na teatralnom fronte" (The new battle on the theatrical front), speech read in Leningrad, 7 Jan. 1929, in RGALI Fonds 998, Opis1, 549.
43 Ibid., 6.
44 Sergey Ignatov, "AKI, GITIS I KAT," in RGALI, Fond 963, Opis 1, 314, 18.
45 Ibid.
46 Meyerhold, *Lektsii 1918–1919*, 25.
47 "Sharlatanstvo ili glupost'" (Charlatanism or stupidity), *Rabochaya Moskva* 196 (3 Nov. 1922), in RGALI, Fonds 963, Opis 1, 314, 3–4.
48 Gilles Deleuze and Félix Guattari, *Capitalisme et Schizophrénie: Mille Plateaux* (*A Thousand Plateaus: Capitalism and Schizophrenia*) (Paris: Éditions de Minuit, 1980).
49 *Die Sexualität im Kulturkampf: zur sozialistischen Umstrukturierung des Menschen* (Copenhagen: Sexpol-Verlag, 1936), translated as *The Sexual Revolution* in 1945 and as *The Discovery of Orgone Vol. 1: The Function of the Orgasm* (New York: Orgone Institute Press, 1942), is perhaps the most infamous.
50 Peter Sloterdijk, "Cell block, egosphere, self-container: The apartment as a co-isolated existence," *Log* 10 (Summer/Fall 2007): 89–108.

Table 3.1 Stanislav Strumilin, "Leisure Time in the Worker's Family – Monthly Budget in Hours per Worker," 1923

Nature of activity	Workers		House-wives	House-hold help	All workers in the family	
	M	F			Sum	%
A. Eating						
1. Tea, breakfast	11.4	8.7	14.3	11.8	11.8	9.1
2. Lunch	18.2	16.0	16.7	15.5	17.1	13.1
3. Dinner	20.3	13.1	21.2	9.9	18.4	14.2
Eating total	49.9	37.8	52.2	37.2	47.3	36.4
B. Leisure activities						
I. Active						
1. Physical						
a) strolling	3.7	3.2	1.4	9.5	3.2	2.5
b) dancing	1.0	4.0	0.6	11.1	2.2	1.7
c) soccer, gorodki, skiing	2.4	–	–	0.9	1.1	0.8
d) hunting	0.5	–	–	–	0.2	0.2
Physical leisure total	7.6	7.2	2.0	21.5	6.7	5.2
2. Aesthetic leisure activities (singing, music)	0.8	5.3	–	–	1.4	1.1
3. Mental (chess, draughts)	1.5	–	0.9	0.2	0.9	0.7
4. Other (cards, lotto)	1.9	1.1	0.5	0.9	1.2	0.9
Active leisure total	11.8	13.6	3.4	22.6	10.2	7.9
II. Passive						
5. Receiving guests	9.8	15.8	7.7	10.0	10.4	8.0
6. Performances (cinema, theatre)	4.5	2.6	2.3	6.9	3.5	2.7
7. Going to church	1.5	3.7	3.1	–	2.4	1.8
8. Visiting tea-rooms, taverns	2.1	–	–	–	0.9	0.7
Passive leisure total	17.9	22.1	13.1	16.9	17.2	13.2

3

A home for a very industrious individual

Living efficiently

How much time do male and female workers, housewives, and household help take to eat breakfast, lunch, and dinner every day? How much time do they spend engaging in "physical," "aesthetic," "mental," and "other" entertainment? Exhaustive answers to these questions appear in a table produced in the early 1920s under the auspices of the Soviet State Planning Commission (known as GosPlan), entitled "Leisure Time in the Worker's Family – Monthly Budgets in Hours Per Worker" (Table 3.1). The table divides workers' activities into two categories: eating and entertainment. Entertainment has two subcategories: active and passive. This presentation of official GosPlan research tells us, for example, that working men spend much more time dining than working women, but housewives eat more slowly than both. Household help spend a lot of time – 9.5 hours a week – strolling. Housewives rarely dance, but the help dances 11.1 hours a week. Women don't seem to play soccer or ski. Working men hunt – 0.5 hours a week. Working women sing – 5.3 hours a week. An average person spends 10 per cent of their time visiting friends, and the working man drinks in a tavern 2.1 hours a week, whereas apparently no one else ever does.

This marvelous research, published in the journal of the Commissariat of Labour, *Voprosy truda* (*Labour Issues*) in 1923, was the brainchild of Stanislav Strumilin. Strumilin was a professor of economics at the Moscow State University and the deputy chief of the State Planning Commission – the institution that planned the economy and life in general. The table represents part of his effort to compile what he called "time-budget studies" (*byudzhety vremeni*) over the course of five years, from 1920 to 1925. The research involved different studies with hundreds of families, resulting in dozens of tables such as the one examined. The table of leisure activities of a family of workers was based on a sample of seventy-six families in Petrograd (later Leningrad), Moscow and Ivanovo-Voznesensk. Strumilin followed the lives of these families over the course of a month, timing everything they did.

This study was followed by a study of office workers whose "domestic labour" Strumilin examined with great precision (Table 3.2). "Domestic labour" involved more intimate activities: the care of hygiene and appearance. Strumilin found that men spend 4.6 hours dressing and undressing, whereas women invest 6.2 hours a month in this activity, and that working women comb their hair for 6.9 hours and housewives 5.2. It seems that working women, with a score of 0.0, never go to the hairdresser, whereas men spend 0.7 hours having haircuts and 2.4 hours shaving. All groups bathe 3 hours a month and swim in the river for 12 minutes. Among Strumilin's studies is one on sleeping and napping. Strumilin established that men nap 1.5 per cent of the day during the working week, and 3.9 per cent on the weekend. Women nap much more than men.

Strumilin explains his intentions:

> Much is now being thought and said about the rationalization, or, as it is now called, the scientific organization of *labour*. But the question of the rationalization of worker's *rest* through the optimal use of his "free" time – this question no one has asked up to now. How could it be asked, when we do not know even the factual distribution of this time and the level of its rationality and irrationality.[1]

To Strumilin, the real puzzle for official science was not factory production but rather life in the home – the mysterious habitat of the Soviet citizen. This puzzle had to be solved because all of life, not only labour in the factory, had to become more rational and efficient. In 1920 Strumilin began measuring and classifying elements of domestic life, which he believed to be akin to production. For him, leisure, self-care, housework, play, were all essentially an expenditure of time and could be therefore streamlined by the government. The motto "Time is Money" should, according to the Soviet economist, be replaced by the motto "Time is Worth more than Money";[2] even those activities that had nothing to do with exchange of money and goods were of economic value.

Table 3.2 Stanislav Strumilin, "Domestic Labour in the Households of Office Workers in 1923–24 (in the number of hours per worker per month)", 1925

	Working men	Working women	House-wives	Help: men	Help: women	Average men	Average women	Average both sexes
Care of self total	**18.3**	**23.7**	**19.3**	**16.0**	**17.3**	**18.1**	**20.7**	**19.6**
Dressing, undressing	4.6	6.2	4.6	2.8	5.4	4.5	5.2	4.8
Washing	5.0	7.0	5.5	5.4	3.7	5.0	5.9	4.4
Combing	2.1	6.9	5.2	2.8	5.8	2.1	5.9	4.4
Having a haircut	0.7	0.0	–	0.6	–	0.7	–	0.3
Shaving	2.4	–	–	0.7	–	2.3	–	0.9
Taking a bath	3.3	3.4	4.0	3.7	2.4	3.3	3.6	3.5
Bathing in the river	0.2	0.2	–	–	–	0.2	0.1	0.1

Strumilin's effort to quantify all non-productive activities, painstakingly timing them, organizing them in tables, and conjuring ways to make them more efficient, was truly obsessive. His enthusiasm for transforming all of life into rational, planned activity akin to labour matched Gastev's enthusiasm for training workers' bodies as machines and attempting to plug them into the great cosmic apparatus. Both were administrator-visionaries, bureaucrat-enthusiasts, who performed government work with great dedication and an apparent dose of lunacy. Gastev's government work translated into a new kind of theatre, theatre in which emotions – excitement – were supposed to be presented by actor-workers by channelling bodily movement so as to present human passions with the "minimal, most purposeful means." Strumilin's science translated into a discourse about the workers' home, in which free time would be modelled after production. His bureaucratic efforts to explore and present the citizen as an individual who is industrious in all spheres of life developed concurrently with architects' efforts to transform the home into a site of labour. Through architecture – the design of everyday spaces and of the object assemblages within them – Soviet citizens were to understand that the principle of life, the principle of all of existence, is efficiency and that all of life should be "rationalized" work.

Every spoon, every nappy, every handkerchief

Strumilin proposes that the material environment plays a crucial role in determining how efficiently and how rationally Soviet citizens spend their time. In his statistical enterprise, determining the time activities such as naps, hunting, undressing, and combing take was only part of the project. At a certain point he observes that there is something more important than the distribution of activities. Everything could, according to him, be explained by studying "the domestic everyday environment [which] produces different tastes and different methods of education in different families."[3] Strumilin describes the environment by describing the presence, number, and distribution of objects. These objects can be counted and classified, and the picture of a worker's private life can thus finally be formed.

Strumilin begins the task of creating a picture of this "domestic everyday environment" by first considering the Soviet statistician's task as similar to that of an archaeologist or palaeontologist. The home is therefore akin to an archaeological site. In "Everyday life and statistics" of 1923, the statistician explains his intentions. "They say that the great natural scientist Cuvier was able to paint the entire evolution of an animal on the basis of a single bone," writes Strumilin. "Studies of primitive culture examine even meagre kitchen leftovers of the caveman and arrowheads [...] of the Stone Age [...] We would like to take as an object of study not only random fossils of everyday life, but the entire complex of things in the worker's everyday life (*byt*) in all its fullness and inviolability."[4]

Critical for Strumilin's entire quasi-paleontological enterprise is the comparison of workers' lives to the lives of "primitive" man in the Stone Age. The workers' quotidian lags behind the Revolutionary epoch and belongs to some other, distant time. How does one prevent servants from dancing so much and men from hunting on the city outskirts? How can women stop spending all their time in the kitchen while men are eating? By not only changing habits and "time budgets," but also understanding and then changing the physical environment in which the workers live, domestic life can be brought forward into the revolutionary present.

Strumilin unearths, counts, combines, classifies, and reclassifies the objects in possession of the Soviet workers in dozens of tables. He gathers together and analyses everything, including "every spoon, every nappy, every handkerchief."[5] He slots them into tables according to different categories, such as use: furniture and decoration; plates and pots; screws, machines, knives and forks, pictures, albums; brushes (with subcategories), scissors, razors, tablecloths, different kinds of handkerchiefs; leather shoes, rubber shoes, clothing and, of course, subcategories of clothing: hats, underwear, coats, shirts, etc. Strumilin establishes how many of them there are, how much they cost, and how long they last.

Driven by his scientific enthusiasm, Strumilin produced tables that could have multiplied to infinity. But the endeavour ended in 1926. The final tables featured objects not according to use but according to material, as if they had just been excavated and nothing of their purpose was known yet. Things are no longer described as samovars, spoons, and combs, but as items of certain materials, akin to Mendeleev's table of elements, describing the makeup of everyday life instead of earth's elements. Strumilin's "environment" consists of wool, felt, cotton, linen, iron and steel, wood, fur, coloured metals, leather, rubber, glass, paper, faience, bristle, and clay. All this is put in a table and quantified, in terms of number per 100 people, price, durability, usability, and overall value (Table 3.3).

Things as co-workers

Strumilin's assertion that it is the physical environment which makes man modern or not – what effectively creates the New Man – and that the physical environment is an assemblage of objects, was not an isolated or eccentric view of a statistician whose enthusiasm for measuring, counting, classifying, and ordering borders on madness. Very similar ideas were developed in Soviet Russia and abroad in the 1920s by architects, artists, and designers. Significantly, the excavations of the "palaeontologist" from GosPlan bear conceptual similarities to the theory of one of the most important art critics of the 1920s, Boris Arvatov, that the transformation of everyday life (*byt*) hinges on adopting a new attitude towards objects.[6]

Strumilin and Arvatov belonged, in a way, to parallel worlds. When Strumilin was working on his time-budget studies, Arvatov was in a psychiatric hospital. At the beginning of the 1920s, he was among the founders of avant-garde art institutions, such as the constructivist group INKhUK and the journal *Lef*. In 1923, however, at the end of the Civil War, when the "building of communism" had just begun, the avant-garde leader disappeared from the public scene, suffering a nervous breakdown. He spent the rest of his life moving from one sanatorium to another. But his enthusiasm survived confinement. From psychiatric sanatoria Arvatov continued to write about art, Soviet society, and the socialist future, as well as about distant America, to which he had never been. These texts were not considered the scribbles of a madman, despite the circumstances in which Arvatov wrote. Because of their rare insightfulness, together with the key role the author had played, and continued to play, in the Russian avant-garde, they were published throughout the decade.

Sentenced to physical and spiritual isolation, surrounded only by objects and fellow sufferers, Arvatov, who was familiar with Meyerhold's work[7] and the concept of "biomechanics," began to examine what can be termed the biomechanical potential of objects – the relationship between the body and the object and the way they "work" together with humans. In "Everyday life and the culture of the thing" of 1925, Arvatov's most well-known work in the English-speaking world,

Table 3.3 Stanislav Strumilin, "Domestic Inventory of Workers in December of 1923 Classified by Material," 1926

Material	Per 100 inhabitants		Average price in rubles	Durability in years		Percentage of Usability of Possessions	Value in rubles per 100 inhabitants	
	Number of items	Sum in rubles		Normal	Factual		In one year	In all years
1. Wool	331.0	2,028.9	6.28	6.7	4.5	31.9	317.2	1,410.0
2. Cotton, linen, etc.	1,397.0	1,636.9	1.17	4.3	2.9	33.4	382.4	1,090.1
3. Iron, cast iron, steel	703.5	1,211.7	1.72	17.9	8.8	52.4	67.5	588.5
4. Wood	533.5	953.3	1.78	15.8	9.0	43.0	60.0	541.1
5. Fur	63.2	594.7	9.39	10.8	6.9	36.0	54.7	379.2
6. Coloured metals	103.2	433.0	4.19	17.2	9/9	42.7	25.1	248.1
7. Leather	97.4	397.9	4.08	3.0	1.9	35.8	133.4	255.2
8. Rubber	52.1	160.5	3.08	2.2	1.5	28.6	72.7	114.4
9. Glass	120.0	144.8	1.21	14.2	7.9	44.5	10.2	80.4
10. Paper	172.9	141.0	0.81	27.0	7.7	71.6	5.2	40.0
11. Porcelain, faience	400.2	109.4	0.27	9.1	5.8	36.4	12.0	69.4
12. Bristle	41.1	16.9	0.41	7.0	3.6	49.2	2.4	8.6
13. Clay	54.0	7.2	0.13	6.0	3.8	37.5	1.2	4.5
14. Other and unknown materials	147.2	509.7	3.45	18.8	10.5	44.7	26.8	281.1
Total	4,216.5	8,395.9	1.99	7.2	4.5	39.2	1,170.8	5,110.6

Arvatov, like Strumilin, proposes that the liberation of the proletariat and the creation of a classless society populated by New Men depend on the transformation of the everyday environment, defined by constellations of things: things that work, that are active. The New Man no longer spends his time in what Strumilin calls "passive entertainment," but relates instead to the world in an active, industrious way.

Arvatov based his ideas on his "observations" of life in America. The fact that he never visited it did not stop him from describing, from his sanatorium room, the American metropolis in great detail. He writes:

> In the city of skyscrapers, of underground and overground metropolitan transit, of mechanized material connections between things, where a thousand transmission apparatuses replace labour – in such a city the inability to manage the thing would mean the total impossibility of existence. The new world of Things, which gave rise to a new image of a person as a psycho-physiological individual, dictated forms of gesticulation, movement and activity. It created a particular regimen of physical culture. The psyche also evolved, becoming more and more thing-like in its associative structure.[8]

Arvatov translates his interpretation of American capitalist modernism to the language of the Revolution. He imagines that all these moving things can be "co-workers" of the proletarian: "The Thing became something functional and active, connected like a co-worker with human practice. Mechanization + dynamization led to the machine-ization of the thing, to its transformation into a working instrument."[9] The worker establishes a "systematically regulated dynamism" of things.[10]

The dynamic home

A Soviet official and a madman; GosPlan and the mental hospital. Strumilin and Arvatov clearly had a common understanding of the environment as an object-assemblage. They also shared an interest in rearranging, transforming, adding, and subtracting objects as a way to, as Arvatov would put it, "dynamize" and "mechanize" everyday life. Strumilin offers a bird's-eye perspective on Soviet life from his position of a high-ranking state employee who has the entire Soviet society in front of him and attempts to mould the Soviet New Man from a position of power. His task is to chart this society, with the goal of inspiring and training the worker to become an efficient creature of the modern age and apply the proletarian work ethic to all aspects of life. Arvatov's perspective is that of a man who, from his location on the margins of power, perceives only glimpses of the brave new socialist world, yet he offers a clear and passionately crafted vision of its future: life in a utopia which he happens to call America, dreaming of a place he never visited as a promised land.

Apart from their common obsession with object-assemblages, the two men share an impracticality of their visions – an impracticality directly proportional to their exuberance. It was up to architects and designers to translate the enthusiasm for creating a factory-like domesticity into more concrete principles for modernizing the material environment. To understand this, one has to turn to the first designs that made the object dynamic, which presented it as an instrument, a "co-worker." The design of an object could transform it and maybe turn it into something that could be used as a tool. These first designs came from VKhUTEMAS, the Higher Art and Technical Studios (see cover letter) the elite Moscow school that had a department for metal design. In 1923, the students of this department exhibited furniture of their own making, which could be "used only in motion, i.e., it is organized as a tool of production."[11] The avant-garde journal *Lef* shows images of beds that turn into an armchair and a coffee table (Figures 3.1, 3.2).[12] Unlike traditional furniture, the students' furniture was easily movable: their designs can change purpose and they also demand a constant active relationship with the inhabitant, who indeed uses them by "operating" them. They demand active physical interaction, that is, domestic labour. Commenting on the achievements of these students three years later, in 1926, the journal *Sovremennaya arkhitektura* (*Contemporary Architecture*) claims that these are "not any kind of things, but things that organize and educate the society."[13] They are things that embody a combination of "productive-constructive and social-organizational skills."[14]

As the 1920s progressed, designers continued to focus on everyday objects with the aim of forming the socialist individual and bringing about a communist way of life. In Chapter 1, I discussed how Vladimir Tatlin, the designer of the Monument to the Third International, turned to portable wings for everyday use. The wings were part of a larger series which included pots, pans, and stoves. Another constructivist, Alexander Toporkov, continued the tradition with furniture that changes shape and purpose, producing sketches of multifunctional

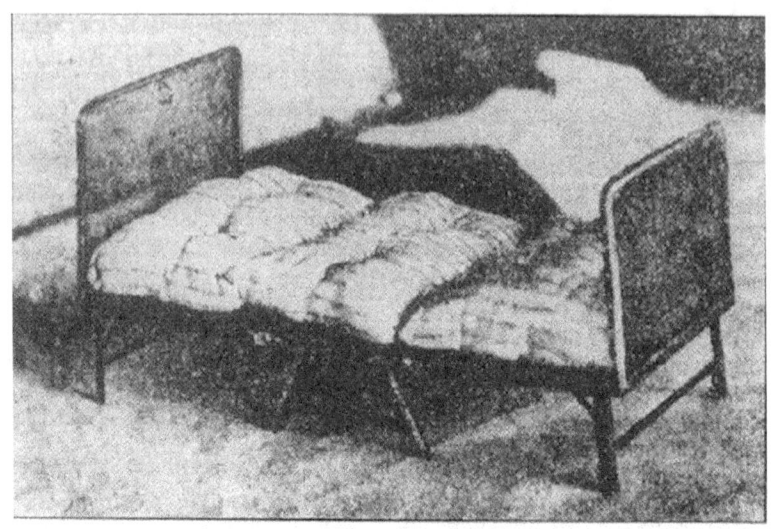

3.1 Petr Galaktionov, folding bed, 1923.

bureaus, folding chairs, an armoire on wheels, and a foldable bed (Figures 3.3, 3.4).

Toporkov complemented his designs with a theory of the object that he presented in *Technical Everyday Life and Contemporary Art*, published in 1928.[15] Like many of his contemporaries, he believed that furniture could influence and transform people. In his book, he introduces Le Corbusier's ideas about the house as a "machine for living" and translates them into a theory of animate objects. "These seemingly obedient and mute slaves," says Toporkov, "which provide us with essential services,

3.2 Nikolay Sobolev, bed-armchair, 1923.

3.3 Alexander Toporkov, furniture design.

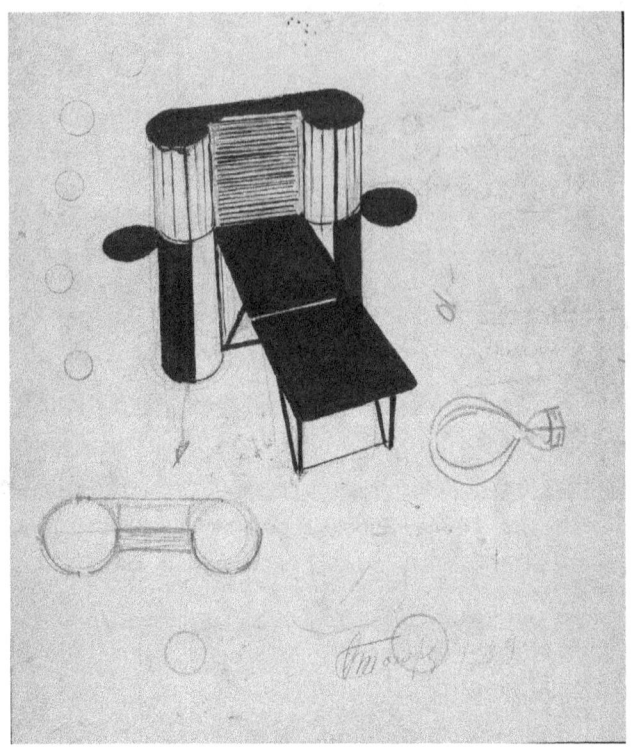

3.4 Alexander Toporkov, sketch for a foldable bed.

also act upon us, force their masters to change, turn them into a different breed of men."¹⁶ Like Arvatov, he turns to distant America and its "mechanized + dynamized" things, such as American furniture – collapsible armoires, rotating shelves, secretaries, registers, calculators – but notes that Americans use these objects only in offices, and not in their homes. In their "personal offices," there are only "leather chairs, sofas, deep as graves."¹⁷ He presents a struggle between the American household and the American office as if it were a Manichean struggle between forces of life and forces of death. In the Soviet Union, he maintains, there will be no difference between the common and the personal office. With the animated object, life will triumph.

Toporkov goes even further in his theory about things having agency: they announce the advent of a new, post-humanist age. Western culture from the Renaissance was the culture of individualist humanism. The

A home for a very industrious individual 79

by Margarete Schütte-Lihotzky, the prototype of all contemporary modular kitchens.[23] Schütte-Lihotzky used standardized elements based on analysis of graphs of movement, trying to make the kitchen as efficient as possible – like a factory (Figure 3.5). The Russian correspondent in *Sovremennaya arkhitektura* is fascinated by the efficiency of Schütte-Lihotsky's design and notices, for example, that the housewife does not cross her hands while cooking.[24]

Almost immediately, that is, in January of 1929, *Sovremennaya arkhitektura* presents the Soviet version of the Frankfurt Kitchen (Figure 3.6). Graphs of movement demonstrate that this kitchen-armoire is

3.5 Margarete Schütte-Lihotzky, Frankfurt kitchen, view.

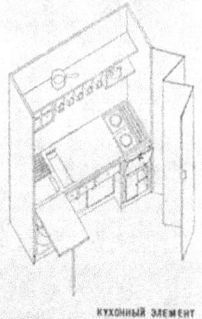

3.6 Article on the rationalized kitchen in *Sovremennaya arkhitektura*, 1929.

more efficient than both the ordinary and the "rationalized" kitchen (Figure 3.7). It occupies only 4.5 square metres but contains all that is needed: a stove, a work surface, sink, pantry, drawers for food and utensils. Like constructivist furniture created in VKhUTEMAS, this object, called a "kitchen element" (*kuhonny element*), is to be treated as an apparatus, folded, unfolded, pulled, pushed, lowered, etc. The journal presents the kitchen element as a "transitional kitchen," which could become an ordinary closet when people began to eat in collective dining halls. This room-object designed to disappear signalled the transition from one type of society to another, from socialism of the present to communism of the future.

The cell

The kitchen element was actually constructed only once, for one of the rare house-communes (*dom-kommuny*), the Dom Narkomfin in Moscow. This commune, in which the majority of domestic activities were supposed to be, but never were, collectivized, was part of a tradition of translating visions of communist domestic life into reality. The most well-known of these is probably the constructivist house-commune designed by Vladimir Vladimirov and Mikhail Barshch the same year Dom Narkomfin was built. Here, the inhabitants were to have common facilities, such as a nursery, gym, and entertainment rooms. In a mechanized dining room all food was to come down an assembly line, and the inhabitants would sit around it and take what they wanted for lunch.

The architects' perspective drawing (Figure 3.8) presents the space of this collective life. But what is interesting is that Vladimirov and Barshch, in addition to collective spaces, presented private proletarian spaces in considerable detail (Figure 3.9). Their design for socialist collectivity began with the "individual unit" of Soviet architecture: minimal personal space. In other words, the individual habitat in the house-commune was as important, if not more so, than collective spaces, because it is in the individual's space that the "domestic office" as envisioned by Toporkov would be established. The most detailed drawings in Vladimirov and Barshch's design, those which received most attention, are those for the "sleeping cabin" (*spalnaya kabina*). The designers provide the dimensions of all elements in the plan. The "cabin" measures 3.75 by 2.6 metres. It contains a work desk (an indispensable part of an "office"),

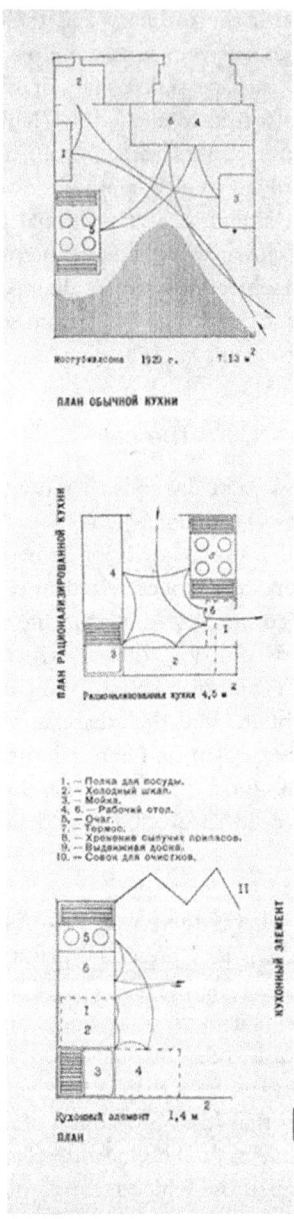

3.7 Plans of the "ordinary kitchen", "rationalized kitchen," and "kitchen element" in *Sovremennaya arkhitektura*, 1929.

A home for a very industrious individual 83

3.8 Vladimir Vladimirov and Mikhail Barshch, experimental project of a house-commune for the Typification Section of the Housing Commission of the RSFR, 1929.

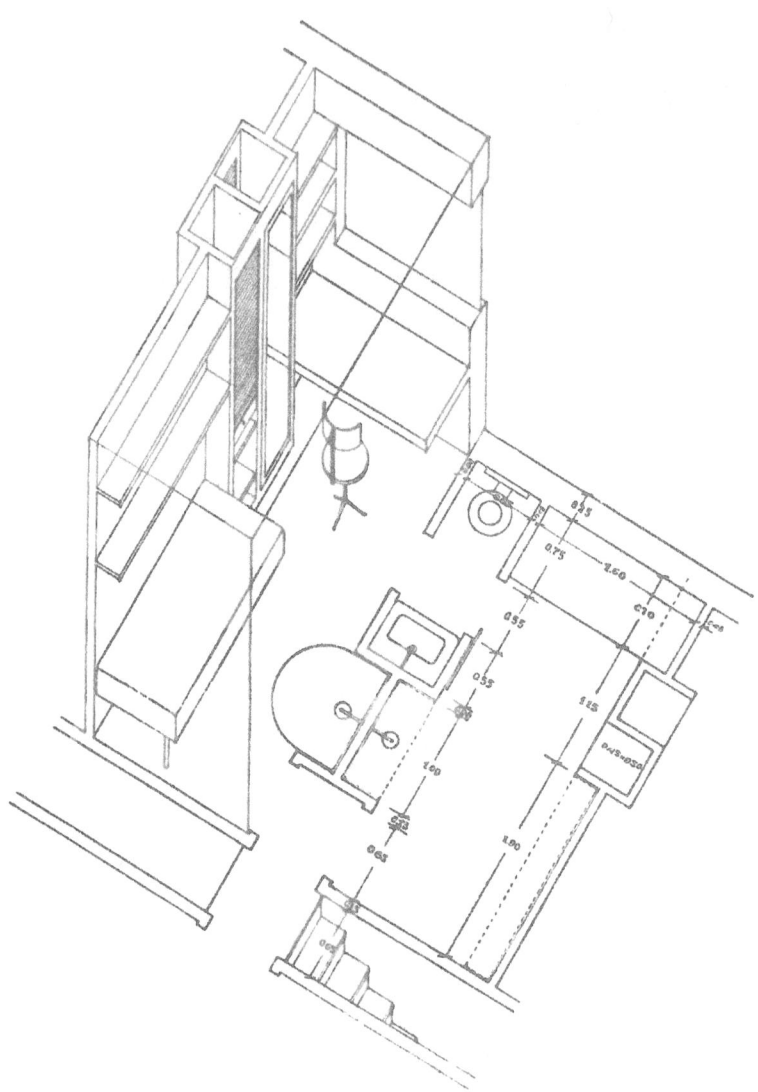

3.9 "Sleeping cabin" (*spalnaya kabina*) in the house-commune by Vladimirov and Barshch, 1929.

a chair, a closet, and a bed. All elements are built into the cabin. Two cabins share a sink and a toilet located between them.

The intent of this cabin was to summon the New Man into being, as the inhabitant of what Toporkov called "non-humanist" space. The person in the sleeping cabin, the minimal and most efficient space, interacts with themself – educates themself, dresses and undresses, showers. These rituals of self-care are not done in the presence of other people but only within the "cabin" itself. The cabin is not divided into the "fixed" space of the architectural envelope and a mobile space for the furniture within. Instead, architecture is the assemblage of these devices of self-care. It is the furniture that is fixed, integrated into the walls and floors; no "personalization" of living space is possible. The interior does not reflect individuality, that which Toporkov called "the internal structure of the I." Instead, the cabin is meant for an impersonal and nomadic inhabitant who "operates" it, rather than leaving a personal imprint by populating it with knick-knacks, rugs, lampshades, and other trappings of bourgeois life.

The new type of architecture also articulates a new relationship between comrades. Individuals are isolated in individual cells and, by eliminating double beds or shared rooms, the architects indicate that, in this ideal world, family as a social institution is destroyed. Instead of sharing a bed, as spouses would do, two individuals in adjacent cells share a toilet. Two units of the collective are connected not by sex but, curiously, by the act of defecation. This was perhaps supposed to connect them in their love for modern hygiene and modern technologies designed for the satisfaction of human needs in general.

In a very similar project, published in 1930, the detailed sleeping unit reappears, albeit in a slightly cleaner form and with better explanations of the ideology behind such a design. Nikolai Milyutin conceived of the ideal city, which he presented in his book *Sotsgorod* (translated as *Socialist City*), a vision of an urban environment in which all urban functions – sleeping, work, leisure, transportation – would be separated and laid out in parallel bands. Like Vladimirov and Barshch, Milyutin devotes most of his attention to the micro-unit, which he names the "living cell" (*zhilaya yacheyka*) (Figure 3.10). It occupies an area of 8.4 metres. As Milyutin explains in his description of the project, he is guided by the idea that the minimal housing unit should not be "reduced to a mere toilet."[25] The living cell features a desk, a folding bed or a bed-sofa, a chair, storage space, and a medicine cabinet. Two

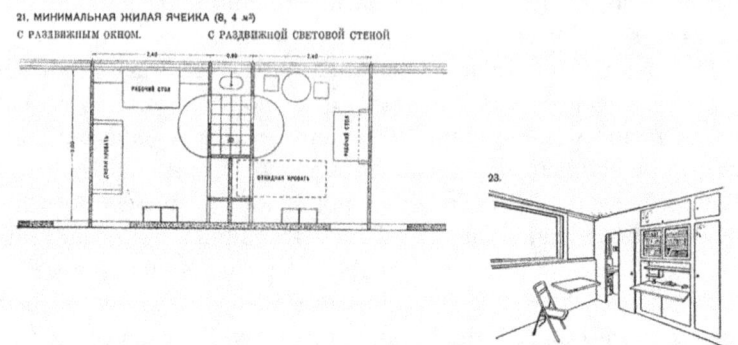

3.10 Nikolay Milyutin, living cell (*zhilaya yacheyka*) in *Sotsgorod*, 1930.

people share a bathroom, which, instead of a toilet contains a sink and a shower.

Milyutin explains that rather than being based on economic interests, these separate cells are meant for individuals who form ties freely. He relates his intent to Karl Marx's idea that it is necessary to eliminate "official and unofficial prostitution," that is, marriage.[26] "In certain circles of the Party," Milyutin explains, "the bourgeois ideology is so strong, that, with a diligence worthy of a less petty purpose, they think up ever new arguments for retaining the double bed as a permanent and compulsory item in the worker's home!"[27]

Instead of the double bed and other bourgeois inventions, Milyutin proposes a house for a worker freed from private property in which "various rags which our inhabitants do so love to 'prettify' their dwelling" would be eliminated.[28] This "dusty accumulation of useless trash" would be replaced by "the minimum necessary equipment that is indispensable for man's living quarters."[29] This equipment consists of an assemblage of parts that the inhabitant manipulates, transforming his "cell" from a day environment into a night environment, from a room for relaxing into a room for reading, etc. In other words, it consists of objects with which the worker collaborates and which, together, constitute a house-mechanism. The inhabitant operates the house-mechanism; for example, by using the "equipment" for bathing and washing hands. Milyutin's proletarian is imagined as a man constantly in action, one who constantly does something in the household, assembling and reassembling his environment, working in it and with it.

Communism's Le Corbusier

The idea of the home as a workplace and habitation as a manipulation of objects was widespread in the Soviet 1920s. Both in harsh Soviet reality and in the visions for house-communes, these spaces were small. People who were to inhabit communist home-workplaces led and were meant to lead an ascetic, almost monastic, life. Projects for house-communes, with their small cells and lavish communal dining rooms, were modelled after monasteries. They were sites of collective dedication to the communist cause. In contrast to these ideas of collective practice of a communist way of life, there were projects in which this kind of life was decentralized and habitation was solitary. Such was a government project in which the workers live an experimental life in "individual houses" (*individual'nye zhilishcha*), responding to the demand for a minimal habitat for Soviet workers. This project belongs to the "disurbanist" movement which emerged in the late 1920s, and was based on the teachings of the Trotskyist sociologist Mikhail Okhitovich. Disurbanist designers thought that ideal proletarian homes were not urban house-communes but groups of individual units, which could be connected in different ways, and should always be situated in nature. One of the projects for such units was Individual House No. 30. Like those previously, this project was developed in close collaboration with government institutions, in this case with GosPlan (led by Strumilin, the inventor of time-budget studies and home inventories) and the Housing Committee of the RSFSR, which in 1930 explored desurbanist ideas in the context of creating housing norms.

For GosPlan, the constructivist group of architects called OSA (*Obedinenie sovremennykh arkhitektorov*, Organization of Contemporary Architects) created a Soviet version of European modernism, a miniature version of Le Corbusier's Villa Savoye (Figure 3.11) which was then being built in France and which was featured in *Sovremennaya arkhitektura* in 1929. The drawing of Individual House No. 30 was published in 1930 in the same journal (Figure 3.12). The Villa Savoye was based on five principles, including strip windows, pilotis which raise the house one level above ground, a free plan, and a roof terrace. The communist villa followed these principles as well. It was raised above ground, had strip windows and a free plan, but no roof terrace. In plan, it measured only 4 by 4 metres.

3.11 Le Corbusier, Villa Savoye, Poissy, France, 1928–1931.

Le Corbusier's design had rooms for servants, a garage, a huge kitchen and living room, three bedrooms, and a boudoir. Individual House No. 30 was a condensed version of Villa Savoye, with only one room. This room was planned as a perfect square (Figure 3.13). The drawings show that it contained a "sanitary-hygienic element" (the sink and toilet), a bed, a table, and a closet, just like the rooms in the house-communes (Figures 3.9, 3.10). In it, the architects tried to use the distribution of objects as the means to define space. They explain this in a bureaucratic language, stating that different configurations of furniture "define various levels of differentiation of everyday functions in the room."[30]

The designs of Toporkov, VKhUTEMAS, Milyutin, and the OSA Group, as well as the design for the kitchen-armoire, all featured the concept of dynamic furniture which the worker would operate and manipulate by moving it, assembling it, disassembling it, opening it, or closing it. The worker literally "works" with his habitat as a one big apparatus, a constant reminder that all life is labour. The designers of the Individual house no. 30, however, move and distribute objects and create different configurations in their imagination, the possibilities manifested only in the drawings. They ccould not decide on a single correct location for the furniture and, for publication, created twelve versions of the same

3.12 OSA, "Individual house no. 30," *Sovremennaya arkhitektura*, 1930.

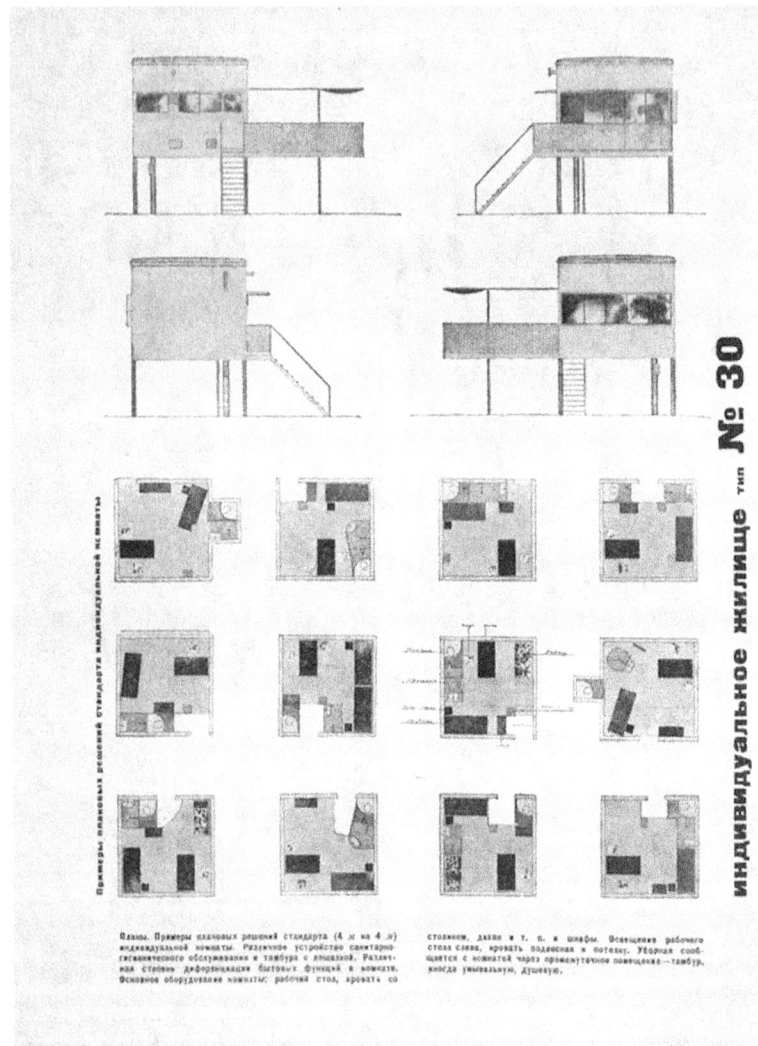

3.13 "Individual House no. 30," facades and twelve plans, in *Sovremennaya arkhitektura*, 1930.

plan, presenting no particular one as ideal. Those "functions" that "radiate" from the bed, closet, table, and the "sanitary-hygienic element" can potentially form an infinite number of constellations. Just as the worker "works" on his habitat, so too does the architect – fascinated with the mobility of things and their capacity to completely determine a way of life – mentally "work" on the magic combination of things that make the home. He operates his design, becoming industrious and productive – a real incarnation of the proletarian New Man.

The Soviet citizen, the labouring self who spends his time at home communicating with objects as his "co-workers" and who is constantly at work organizing them, connecting them, setting them into action, is also the image of the architect. The act of design is, in part, the act of assembling and reassembling things, in this case not just in the finished habitat but also on the drawing board.

Postscript

It is not surprising that the critique of productivism and "rationalization," as pursued by the government and by architects in the rather chaotic and sometimes surreal 1920s, was the critique of "working" with objects. What the designer Toporkov called *predmentost*, or "object-mindedness," became a poetic device of a group called OBERIU (Association of Real Art) that explored socialist life as the theatre of the absurd. Members of this group rendered ludicrous the tragi-comic interpretations of the Soviet quotidian that statisticians, architects, and art critics set out to reform. The proclaimed principle guiding the work was also *predmentost*, which they defined as "a new feeling for life and objects."[31] Perhaps the most prominent member of this group was Danil Harms, whom one critic called "the chronicler and the troubadour of the trivial, the everyday, the normal."[32] Harms associated words together to create "chains" of objects, thus representing the world as a chain reaction of things and thoughts. An example is his story, "Petya Gvozdikov," which goes like this:

> Petya Gvozdikov once walked around his apartment. He was very bored. He picked up a piece of paper dropped by the maid from the floor. The paper turned out to be a cutout from the newspaper. This was not interesting. Petya tried to catch the cat, but the cat hid under the cupboard. Petya went to the foyer to get an umbrella, to chase the cat with the

umbrella from under the cupboard. But when Petya came back, the cat was not under the cupboard any more. Petya looked for the cat under the sofa and behind the trunk, but he did not find it anywhere, but he found instead a hammer behind the trunk. Petya took the hammer and started to think what to do with it. Petya began banging on the floor with the hammer, but that was boring. Then Petya remembered that on the chair in the foyer is a little box of nails. Petya went to the foyer, took a couple of thicker nails from the box and started thinking about where to drive them. If the cat were there, it would of course be interesting to nail the cat's ear to the door, and the tail to the threshold. But the cat was not there. Petya saw the piano. And, out of boredom, Petya went and drove three nails into the lid of the piano.[33]

There apparently is no reason for connecting things to one another, for Petya Gvozdikov to create the object-assemlage that Harms describes. Architects' and bureaucrats' rational efforts to "dynamize" the home are mirrored in Harms' domestic scene. Rather than by revolutionary enthusiasm, Petya Gvozdikov is driven by boredom. What Strumilin calls "passive entertainment" is simply the ennui of the ordinary citizen. In utopian vision, in the radiant future populated by efficient, working proletarians, domestic life involves "working" with objects – manipulating them, moving them, connecting them to each other. But the domestic life of Harms's bored and frustrated protagonist of the socialist present also involves constantly picking something up, putting something down, hitting things, imagining hitting things. Both the ideal socialist citizen and the one who is bored and exasperated by life's meaninglessness treat the home as as an assemblage of objects, of "coworkers." The idealistic vision of domesticity as efficient and purposeful, representative of the dynamism and marvels of the modern age, strangely reflects a vision that presents it as grim and absurd. In radically different representations of Soviet life, domestic environments are essentially in a constant state of construction and deconstruction, of unfinishedness, as opposed to the fixed, static life of another time and place. As are their inhabitants.

The communist home is is not a house. It is an object-assemblage for performing chains of activity akin to labour in the factory. Unlike the design of theatrical or urban space, the design of domesticity was about articulating the identity of the New Man as an individual, though not in the manner of "individual humanism." It was based on the notion that objects and people – the New Men – exist together, on the same plane, and interact "with" each other, instead of individuals acting "upon" the material world according to their personal motivations. Domesticity, envisioned as constant labour in the home, was the constant interaction between the animate and the inanimate. It was the repeated act of merging with the world – the materialist version of *bytie*, of transcendence. It could happen in the throes of productive enthusiasm. It could happen while shaving and dressing. And it could happen while bored to tears.

Designers, poets, and bureaucrats considered the Soviet home a milieu – a technically enhanced environment of bodies, things, devices, and substances. Whereas "humanist" design differentiated between the man and the walls of a house, here the inhabitant is part of a system of matter and devices, is immersed in it. The next chapter explores the development of this idea on a much larger scale, and at the ultimate site of immersion – the public bathhouse and its accretion of liquids, vapours, bodies, materials, and machines.

Notes

1 "Byudzhet vremeni russkogo rabochego v 1922 g" (The time budget of the Russian worker), orig. in *Voprosy truda*, no. 3–4 (1923), reprinted in S. G. Strumilin, *Problemy ekonomiki truda* (*Problems of Labour Economy*) (Moscow: Gosudarstvenoe izdatelstvo politicheskoi literatury, 1957), 269.
2 Ibid.
3 "Byt i statistika" (Everyday life and statistics), written in 1923, first published in Strumilin, *Problemy ekonomiki truda*, 234.
4 "Byt i statistika," in Strumilin, *Problemy ekonomiki truda*, 393–394.
5 "Domashny byt po inventaryam" (Domestic everyday life according to inventories), in Strumilin, *Problemy ekonomiki truda*, 365, originally published as "Rabochii byt v tsifrakh" (Workers' life in numbers), in *Statistiko-ekonomicheskie etyudy* (Moscow-Leningrad: Planovoe khozaistvo, 1926).
6 The work of Arvatov has been introduced to the English-speaking world by Christina Kiaer, who published translations of his "Byt i kultura veshchi" from *Almanakh Proletkulta* (Moscow, 1925) in the journal *October* as "Everyday life and the culture of the thing (toward the formulation of the question)," no. 81 (Summer 1996): 119–128. Kiaer also based her research on Soviet constructivism on his writing. See Christina Kiaer, *Imagine No Possessions: The Socialist Objects of Russian Constructivism* (Cambridge: MIT Press, 2008). For Kiaer, the theory of the object is of key importance to Russian avant-garde art. She focuses on the notion of property and the somewhat

anthropomorphic characteristics of the object, which she calls "psychological transparency." It is worth complementing her work by extending this discussion beyond the confines of constructivist art and as part of the broader discussion of labour as it guided the comprehensive transformation of domestic spaces in the Soviet 1920s.

7 He examines Meyerhold's work in "Teatr kak proizvodstvo" (Theatre as production) in *Ob agit i proz isskustve*, 137, originally in *Gorn*, 1 no. 6 (1922) and in "Ot rezhissury teatra k montazhu byta" (From theatre directing to the montage of everyday life) *Ob agit i proz isskustve* (Moscow: Izdatel'stvo "Federatsiya," 1930), 158, orig. *Zrelishcha*, 24 (1923).
8 Arvatov, "Everyday life and the culture of the thing," 126.
9 Ibid.
10 Ibid., 128.
11 Varvara Stepanova, "O rabotakh konstruktivistkoi molodezhi" (On the work of constructivist youth), *Lef*, 3 (1923): 56.
12 Ibid., 53.
13 *Sovremennaya arkhitektura*, no. 3 (May 1929): 121.
14 Ibid.
15 Alexander Toporkov, *Tehnichesky byt i sovremennoe isskustvo* (*Technical Everyday Life and Contemporary Art*) (Moscow and Leningrad: Gosudarstvennoe Izdatel'stvo, 1928).
16 Ibid., 92–93.
17 Ibid., 44.
18 Ibid., 23.
19 Ibid., 30.
20 Ibid., 96–97.
21 Ibid., 97.
22 Mark Grigor'evich Meerovich, *Kak vlast narod k trudu priuchala: Zhilishche v SSSR—sredstvo upravleniya lyud'mi 1917–1941 gg.* (*How the Government Taught People to Work: Housing in USSR as Means of Controlling People 1917–1941*) (Stuttgart: Ibidem-Verlag, 2005).
23 L. Jacobson, "The Frankfurt kitchen," *Sovremennaya arhitektura*, 5 (1928): 166.
24 Ibid., 166.
25 Nikolai A. Milyutin, *Sotsgorod: The Problem of Building Socialist Cities*, trans. Arthur Sprague (Cambridge: MIT Press, 1974), 82.
26 Ibid., 77.
27 Ibid.
28 Ibid., 84.
29 Ibid., 84, 81.
30 "Individual House No. 30," *Sovremennaya arkhitektura*, no. 6 (November 1930): 13.

31 In *Oxford Slavonic Papers*, New Series, no. 3 (1970): 69–73, orig. in *Afishi doma pechati*, no. 2
32 George Gibian, "Introduction," in Danil Harms, *Izabrannoe*, ed. George Gibian (Wurzburg: Jal-verlag, 1974), 37.
33 Translation mine. Russian text accessed online, *Lib. Ru: Biblioteka Maxima Moshkova*. http://www.lib.ru/HARMS/xarms_prose.txt, accessed 19 May 2015.

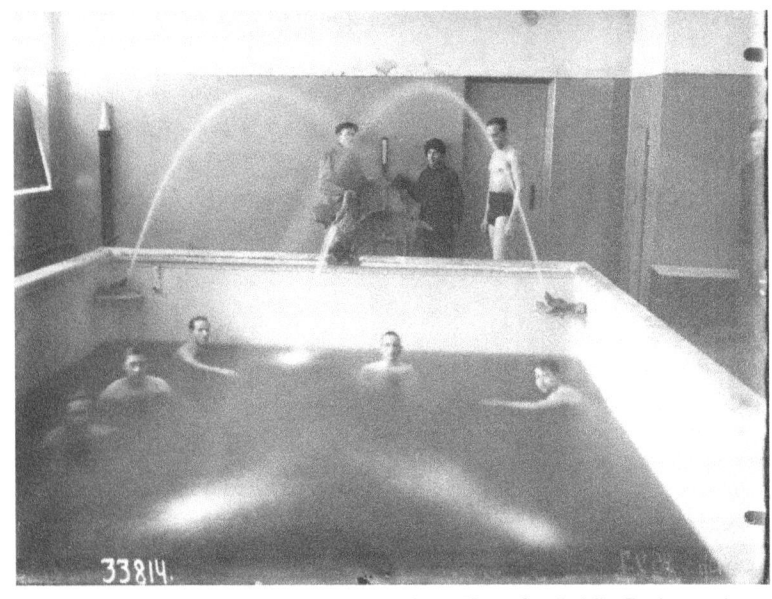

4.1 A group of men in the pool of the Trust for Public Baths and Laundries, Leningrad 1932.

4

The world in the bathhouse, the bathhouse in the world

The building that works

On a winter day in 1932, five men in Leningrad immerse themselves in an indoor pool. Another man in swimming trunks stands behind the pool beside two men in coats who seem to be in charge of heating (Figure 4.1). Everyone faces the camera. Two crisscrossing jets emerge from the gaping mouths of cast iron frogs nestled in the corners of the pool. An iron swan captured in half flight emits a short and forceful spray. The two pool operators next to the thermometer point proudly to the display, which shows the perfect temperature of the water.

This photograph, taken in the Leningrad Trust for Public Baths and Laundries by an anonymous photographer, is a record of a beautiful and efficient enclosed environment, a perfectly functioning little world of pleasure and camaraderie. The picture is also a record of a design that, unlike many other things in Soviet everyday life, worked like magic. It comes from an era in which projects for bathhouses and spaces of hygiene, as well as the precision with which these environments were regulated, became a vehicle for bringing the ethics of planned economy literally close to the citizen's skin. In such spaces of hygiene, the relationship between the body and the State was performed in a way that reflected the ethos of the industrialized and collectivized world of the Soviet 1930s. Buildings that worked had finally, around 1930, supplemented the working bodies and working objects of the 1920s, discussed in previous chapters. These buildings presented the efficiency and beauty of the evolving industrialized world and articulated the identities of those who lived in it.

Before moving on to understand how buildings and, implicitly, the Soviet system of the 1930s worked, it is worth considering how things did not work. In his story, "Bathhouse," written in 1924, the Russian writer Mikhail Zoshchenko relates his attempt to take a bath in one of Leningrad's *banyas* – public facilities for bathing and steaming the body and doing laundry.[1] Zoshchenko never succeeds in his attempt. He only encounters the representatives of petty bureaucracy and finds himself immersed in the chaos of Leningrad's civic life. Zoshchenko undresses at the entrance to the *banya*, hands his clothes to the superintendents and gets two tickets, one for his coat and one for the rest of his clothing. He then walks through the *banya* in his birthday suit, the two tickets tied around his ankle. The *banya* is crowded. Despite a long and thorough search, he cannot find a bucket to wash himself. "The hell with everyone," he concludes. "I will finish bathing at home." But this is where trouble begins. "I go back to the locker room," he describes. "I give them one ticket. They give me my linen. I look. Everything is mine, but the trousers aren't mine. 'Citizens', I say, 'mine didn't have a hole here. Mine had a hole over there.' But the attendant goes, 'We aren't here,' he says, 'just to watch for your holes.'"[2] Zoshchenko manages to identify and reattach himself to his wardrobe by identifying clothes with holes in the right places and with the correct number of detached buttons. He survives his participation in collective life and the interaction with the representatives of officialdom with some effort.

Zoshchenko's story was published half a decade before the topic of public *banyas* was addressed, in 1930, by Ivan Kudryakov, a correspondent of the journal *Culture and Everyday Life* (*Kul'tura i byt*).[3] The "culture" in the journal's title refers to sober life, and the journal was dedicated to the battle against alcoholism. It included proposals for alternative ways of spending free time and introductions to new institutions for this purpose. One of the most important "cultural" institutions in this journal, in addition to cinemas and workers' clubs, was the reformed public *banya*. Kudryakov reports on his visit to the newly built Proletarian *Banyas* (*Proletarskie bani*) in Moscow, which he calls "the palace of health." In this "palace" the newly minted worker-aristocrat doesn't have to stand in line, fight for buckets, and rub shoulders with other bathers, and, instead of having his coat lost, he retrieves it washed and pressed. The *banya* has a gigantic pool and an automated laundry, and the worker and his attire are cleaned in a magically swift and smooth manner. "I took off my dirty underwear, handed it in, and went for a swim. During the time I washed myself and swam, time passed, I came back to the waiting room and my underwear was waiting for me, clean and ironed."[4]

The two texts, one about Leningrad in 1924 and the one about Moscow in 1930, describe two worlds, two different stages of public life. In one, disorder, arrogance, and misrecognition rule, and its protagonist can account for nothing but holes and missing buttons. The other is efficient, clean, and apparently palatial. The writer of the first piece is a cynic; he experiences the public bath as pandemonium ruled by incompetent administrators, a symbol of the mess that is Leningrad. The correspondent of *Culture and Everyday Life* is an admirer of the mechanical efficiency of service. He surrenders to the precise workings of this instrument of self-care provided by the socialist State, indulges in them, and describes them with passion and fascination. In the Soviet *banya*, which Kudryakov calls "the palace of health," he is meant to turn from beggar to prince. Once he is cleansed and transformed, he enters the bright new age of sobriety and efficiency, imbued with the virtue of order.

The drastic difference between the two accounts is not only the difference of genre, the difference between a literary account and journalistic persuasion. It is also a difference in era. Zoshchenko's story is written during the era of the New Economic Policy (NEP), between 1921 and 1928, which Lenin characterized as a time when the Soviet Union "took one step back in order to move two steps forward." Small trade and small-scale private ownership were permitted and the economy was not entirely collectivized. Industrial production on a large scale remained a dream due to technological backwardness and the absence of consolidation of industrial facilities. The journal *Culture and Everyday Life* appeared at the cusp of the 1930s, the time of Stalin's First Five-Year Plan (1928–1932), which was characterized by large-scale industrialization and the collectivization of the economy, in which the power of the socialist State grew exponentially with the acceleration of the industrialization process.

The number of *banyas* built and renovated around 1930 was relatively small. In Moscow and Leningrad, between 1928 and 1932, only six were constructed and two renovated.[5] These new *banyas* did not significantly improve the everyday life of the proletariat. Access to bathing facilities in Moscow and Leningrad was still limited, to say the least, with *banyas* providing perhaps one bath a month for each citizen.[6] But despite being few, these projects were featured and discussed in the media, in both popular and professional literature, as the ultimate achievement in revolutionizing Soviet everyday life and emancipating the proletariat. In particular, the *banya* was intended to provide new forms of socialization: collective rituals of self-care linked to inherent qualities of industrial production, such as efficiency and precision.

The *banya* as an idea: water, steam and collectivity

The story of the Soviet public bathhouse around 1930 is a story of the transformation of the *banya*, an age-old institution, an indispensable element of Russian everyday life – and an object of government speculation that predates the communist era. The *banya* is, first and foremost, an idea, rather than an architectural type. The *banya* could be a shack in the country consisting of a steam room that would be followed by the individual jumping into snow, ice or a river. It could also be an elaborate urban structure, with pools of various temperatures, ice-cold tubs, and tearooms for relaxing after a sweat and a swim. There were fancy "first class" *banyas* and those of "second class," which often had sinks for doing laundry for those who did not have running water at home. In all cases, and throughout its history, the *banya* was conceived of as a place dedicated to cleansing the whole body, inside and out, as well as the spirit. It was also imagined as a site where people socialized without clothes, forming temporary communities of naked, occasionally indulgent and often excited individuals. Men and women subjected their bodies to extreme alterations of temperature, moving between the extreme heat of the sauna and the extreme coolness of water, or, in rural bathhouses, snow and ice outside the steamed room.[7] This was supposed to rejuvenate and heal. The *banya* not only cured the body, however; it was also a proto-communist space, a liminal space at the edges of society in which relationships of power and social hierarchies were temporarily abolished in collective nudity. "In the banya there are no epaulettes," the proverb goes; "in the banya all are equal." Stripped not only of their tokens of rank, the bathers entered a community of equals.

The long-held conception of the bathhouse as a means of corporeal and spiritual cleansing, the fountain of youth and longevity, persisted into modern times. The image of the bathhouse as a zone of social equality, however, was modified to involve the intervention of State authorities. The discourse on the *banya* served in many cases to legitimize their power by presenting it as emancipatory. It is symptomatic, for example, that around the turn of the twentieth century, a certain N. A. Goldenberg, "the doctor of the twenty-fifth infantry division," penned a medical treatise about baths. Titled *The Bath for Armies and Popular Masses*, the treatise offers advice on establishing baths that should be established by anyone – doctors, military officers, government, schools, factories – members of institutions of any kind as well as the administrators of those institutions.[8] Goldenberg presents two main ideas. The first is that the *banya* should become a device for demonstrating that the State treats all citizens equally by providing them with the same essential service. It is the need for bathing that makes all men equal, and institutions should make sure that "people's baths" should "be made and organized in such a way that every man, independent of his class or rank"[9] has access to it free of cost. Goldenberg's second idea is that, by organizing baths, the State not only enlightens but also disciplines its subjects. He likens the provision of bathing facilities to "the care of the father for the health of the family";[10] the "masses" are a "big child" that has to be coaxed to practise hygiene and to "rationally understand what is to its own benefit."[11] The model for the bathhouse is now curiously the military – bathing enlightens and educates because it is carefully regimented – scripted and timed, described as "gymnastics for muscles and nerves and a system for regulating our organic temperature" that "insures the organism against every kind of danger."[12]

This idea did not catch on in Imperial Russia, but the blueprint for the modern public bathhouse was to be realized during the First Five-Year Plan (1928–1932). The double idea that the *banya* is a symbol of equality and civic unity and that it is a demonstration of State care for the citizenry and its enlightening role was first tested in projects for bathhouses that emerged immediately after the Revolution. In 1919, a competition for public "thermae" in Petersburg, which were to replace the old imperial castle, was organized by the Artistic Committee of the Architectural Studio of the All-Union Council for Municipal Economy (*Khudozhestvenny Sovet Arkhitekturnoy Masterskoy SovKomHoz*). The winning entry, by Noah Trotsky and his team, though never built, was a classicist project, modelled on ancient Roman architecture and urbanism, for a bathhouse of an enormous scale, with showers, pools, stadia, and a skating rink.

However, during the 1920s no major attempts were made to actually build such colossal *banyas*. In addition, *banyas* were not yet completely collectivized, operated instead by private renters. The new type of *banya* – the type that fitted the description of the Soviet "palace of hygiene" and demonstrated both care for the worker and technological progress in the era of collectivized economy – began to emerge in the 1930s. This is when the State placed most other public institutions under its control, after the private renters and managers of urban bathing facilities were "unmasked" as capitalists; the State took over bathhouse facilities for the sake of the "people's health."[13] As part of the collectivization project during the First Five-Year Plan, the government takeover of public *banyas* also entailed the construction of new flagship buildings to demonstrate the new order of self-care within a proletarian collective life.

The *banya* as a site of production

The implementation of new technologies and their integration into processes of self-care defined the truly Soviet bath, of the kind that would radically improve the life of the workers. Between 1930 and 1932, in addition to the story about the proletarian *banya* in *Culture and Everyday Life* discussed earlier, articles proliferated on the symbolic and technical connection between the industrial plant and the *banya*. A prominent platform for discussing the mechanization of self-care was the Leningrad *Voprosy kommunalnogo khozyaystva* (*Problems of Municipal Economy*). This journal, published by the Advertising Trust of the Leningrad Regional Department of Municipal Economy from 1924 to 1932, features a great number of impassioned articles whose goal was to demonstrate that "the pace of building new everyday life" follows "the pace of industrialization of industrial and agricultural economy."[14] The main characteristic of the *banya* as an architectural type, as presented in *Problems of Municipal Economy*, is not any not formal design feature but rather the presence of machines that modernize the functions of the bathhouse, such as heaters and ironing and washing machines (Figures 4.2, 4.3).

Communal industrial laundries, which in this period had become part of the public bathhouse, occupy a prominent place in the journal. In 1931 a nine-page article entitled "Social and communal laundries" discussed the process of washing linen as being identical to that of

The world in the bathhouse 103

4.2 "Washing machine," *Problems of Municipal Economy*, 1931.

factory production and a logical development of the modernization of bathing and the modern approach to sanitation and hygiene.[15] The article features plans of laundries as houses for machines and discusses the ultimate distribution of these machines in space for greater efficiency. The process of doing laundry is dissected, in the vein of Taylorism, into components of the process, which are assigned different architectural environments, such as receiving dirty laundry, sorting, washing, drying, ironing, storage, distribution, and delivery of clean clothes. The architecture of the laundry is discussed in terms of the portion of the floor surface dedicated to each of these functions and technical requirements for each step of the production process, including recommendations for ventilation, light, floor and wall surfaces, temperature regulation, cost of the facility, water consumption, and

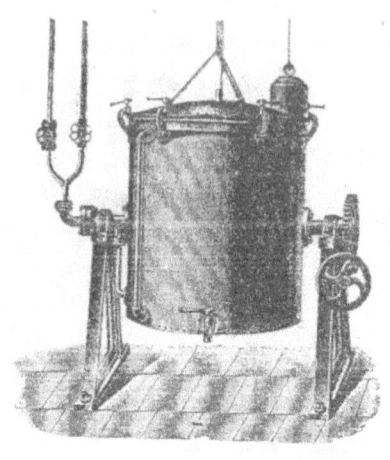

4.3 "Boiler and conveyor belt for laundries," *Problems of Municipal Economy*, 1931.

4.4 Nikolay Demkov, *Banya* on 3 Stantsionnaya Street, c. 1930 (photo 1934).

dimensions of the facility in proportion to the weight of the laundry it processes. The article presents mathematical formulas for calculating necessary number and capacity of machines, square footage, etc.

Photographs such as that of the *banya* on Stantsionnaya Street in Leningrad (Figure 4.4) indicate the "industrial" nature of the public bathhouse. The *banya* in the photograph, designed around 1930 by Nikolay Demkov, is presented with its technical counterpart – the heating plant. The plant and the public bathhouse are not only situated next to each other, they are alike by design. They are built of the same brick, the curvature of the full-height corners of the bathhouse mirrors the curvature of the tall plant chimney, and the surface of both buildings is devoid of ornament. In addition, the presence of the modern heating plant, which replaces traditional sources of heat, next to the bathhouse announces that popular health, hygiene, and pleasure now belong to the industrial age and that the government as the manager of modern industry (including this heating facility) is in charge of providing for the wellbeing of the masses.

What was the relationship between the bather and the machinic architecture that surrounded him? An answer to this question can be found in the description in *Culture and Everyday Life* at the beginning of this chapter, of a visit to a *banya* in 1930. What the worker as a visitor to the bathhouse experiences is not kinship with machines as his "co-workers," unlike the experience of the worker using the machine that was the one-room abode in the 1920s, and unlike the interaction of actor with actor and with the biomechanical theatre stage. The visitor to the *banya* does not experience an active relationship to the building – does not "operate" the apparatus that is the bathhouse. To the contrary, the bather is passive, "processed" by the building. He is the product of the building as a plant for manufacturing hygiene.

This notion is articulated not only in propaganda from the period but also in the name of one of the baths, a renovation of an old bath in the Leningrad Vasileostrovsky District (Figure 4.5). In 1931, the old Gavanskie *banya* was replaced with a building called the "Sanitary Conveyor of the Vasileostrovsky District" (*Sanpropusnik vasileostrovskogo rayona*). The name of the building indicates that its purpose is to produce a clean citizen, as if on a production line. The exterior of the

4.5 Alexander Gegello: Sanitary Conveyer of the Vasileostrovsky District, 1931.

building suggests what appears to be a different message. The front facade is monumental in both size and design. The centre of the massive brick wall is pierced by four thin vertical slits, producing an effect of heaviness, as if the building were made of stone. In fact, the overall composition seems to have been modelled not after a factory but after an Egyptian pylon.

Life, death, and the working-class body

How to interpret this choice of historical reference? Whereas Greek and Roman motifs informed the vocabulary of the classicist architects who designed institutional buildings in this period, the Egyptian pylon was an acceptable reference for their modernist counterparts because of its clear massing and lack of elaborate ornamentation. The monumentality of the facade of the "conveyor" also articulates the stability and power of the State that brings about progress and introduces high technology not only into industrial production but also into everyday life. The fascinating combination of the industrial and the monumental in the *banya* manifests the programme of the First Five-Year Plan – economic development and the solidification of government power, both of which entailed the creation of a new "processed" subject.

The machinism of the 1930s seems to be quite different to the machinism of the 1920s; in the 1920s, the proletarian was the operator of the environment, while around 1930, the proletarian became its product. In the "processing" and production of the new citizen in buildings such as the "sanitary conveyor," not only was the citizen's body cleansed but it was also manipulated, in all its physical and metaphysical states; its flows of energy and matter, which defined embodied existence, managed. In the same year, 1931, that the *banya* in the Vasileostrovsky District was completed, Gegello, with Krichevsky, presented a project in *The Problems of Municipal Economy* for a crematorium, with a facade similar to that of his Leningrad *banya*, an elaboration on the Egyptian pylon (Figure 4.6). There is both a conceptual and an administrative connection between the *banya* and the crematorium. The idea of using the bathhouse as a crematorium was not alien to the Soviet post-Revolutionary administration. The first Leningrad facility for cremation (the communist alternative to church burial) was established in 1921 in the *banya* of the Vasileostrovsky District.[16] The attempt was not a great success, and lasted only a couple of months. But the concept resurfaced

4.6 Gegello and Krichevsky, "Design for a crematorium," *Problems of Municipal Economy,* 1930.

in 1959, when baths and crematoriums were treated as one entity in city planning.[17] Both establishments, so similar in appearance in Gegello's design, were together intended to process both the living and the dead proletarian body, and to guide the way the citizen negotiates his relationship to its ephemerality and fragility, as well as define the transition from life to death, an area on which the Orthodox Church once provided guidance.

The *banya* as a threshold between life and death, between dirt and purity, entailed recycling bodily matters and integrating bodily substances into the building itself within a discrete closed ecosystem. In 1932, a year after Gegello's Sanitary Conveyor was built, the People's Council for Municipal Economy proposed a system of product "regeneration" to be implemented in all *banyas* so as to incorporate various kinds of organic refuse into a system. The details of the system were outlined in a document called "On the Intensification of Works on Extracting and Utilizing Waste Products in Bathhouse and Laundry Management."[18] The document identifies ways to use products of a bathhouse:

> People's Council for Municipal Economy [NarKomKhoz], in cooperation with scientific and research institutes, approached the investigation of these issues:
>
> 1. the regeneration, collection and utilization of soap from processed bath and laundry water
> 2. the use of heat in bath water
> 3. the use of human hair from hair salons as mix in felt used for construction.[19]

The naked women and men in the building were not only rejuvenated but in a sense recycled, their hair embedded in the *banya* building.

Baptism under the communist dome

The *banya* was both a bubble of communist collective intimacy and an ecosystem in which the intimate relationship between the body and the building defined the subject of Soviet industrialization. It was an efficient mechanism, a machine for "processing the citizen" and a machine for spreading productivist ethos – the enthusiasm for the machine. But it was also a representation – a microcosmic rendering of the world as ordered by the First Five-Year Plan; a building that encapsulated the order of the communist universe in becoming. Rituals of self-care were also rituals by which the beauty, efficiency and harmony of the planned socialist world were observed. Formally, this microcosmic character of the public bath is nowhere better articulated than in a particular type – the round *banya*.

The potential of the *banya* as a site of physical and spiritual transformation and rapture inspired enthusiasm in architects. The most excessive and fantastic interpretation of the *banya* as a microcosm was that of Alexander Nikolsky, who transformed this building type into a veritable communist temple. Intentionally or unintentionally, he established in his design a clear formal link between the *banya* as a socialist microcosm and the Russian church as a celestial microcosm; the rituals of hygiene that were supposed to take place in them were also mystical rituals similar to those of the Orthodox religion.

Nikolsky's first and unbuilt project, conceived in the late 1920s, at the very end of the period of New Economic Policy, is a colossal round *banya* intended for Leningrad (Figure 4.7). It is most akin to a

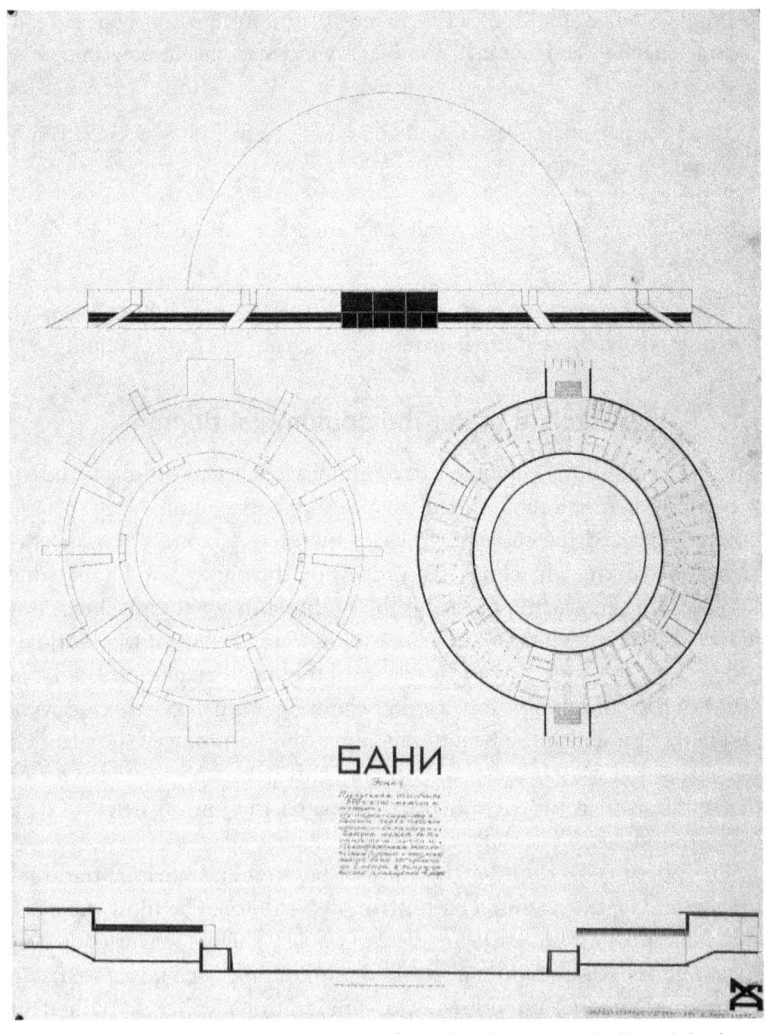

4.7 Alexander Nikolsky, project for a bathhouse, unbuilt, original drawing, 1927.

spaceship. At the same time, the most important element of design, the large dome, resembles that of an Orthodox church, envisioned as a small replica of the world in which the dome is meant to represent the heavens. In the centre of the *banya* is a swimming pool 54 metres across. The dome is equipped with a mechanism that allows it to open and close, in response to weather conditions. According to the plans, the building consists of an outer ring, sunbathing decks on the roof, and steaming and showering facilities below. The ring is divided into two halves, one for men and one for women, with separate entrances. In each half, facilities for undressing, steaming, and bathing are laid out in succession, in two different "classes," or levels of luxury, for each sex. The capacity of the building is huge – it can process 4,000 bathers a day, or 500 bathers an hour. These hundreds of bathers would collectively immerse themselves into the gigantic pool, in a socialist version of baptism. However, here collective belonging would be characterized not by love of God but by love of hygiene, taking place under a mechanized firmament.

The singularity of the pool building and its status as a ritual territory was underscored by its peculiar relationship to the terrain. The building is not level with the site. Dressing, showering, and steaming facilities are buried 2 metres below ground, and the solarium on the roof is just two metres above ground, tied to the land only by thin ramps that lead to the deck. The building is intentionally separated from the ground – elevated above it and buried below it. Its round plan, the circle being the articulation of self-containment, further contributes to its status as a ritual site, detached from the space of ordinary, everyday urban life.

This was perhaps an eccentric project, but one celebrated in the architectural literature of the time as a model socialist building of the post-Revolutionary age. In *Architecture for World Revolution*, published in 1930, El Lissitzky presents Nikolsky's *banya* as an example of a building that is "no longer private and intimate" but exemplifies "the public and the universal," being "tied to economic problems."[20] On the list of significant buildings that embody the striving for the "universal" are the Palace of Labour of 1923, by the Vesnin brothers, their Leningradskaya Pravda of 1924, and Konstantin Melnikov's Soviet Pavilion at the 1925 World Fair. Examples of revolutionary architecture also include housing communes and workers' clubs. Nikolsky's building is an example of progressive architecture applied to the realm of what El Lisstizky calls

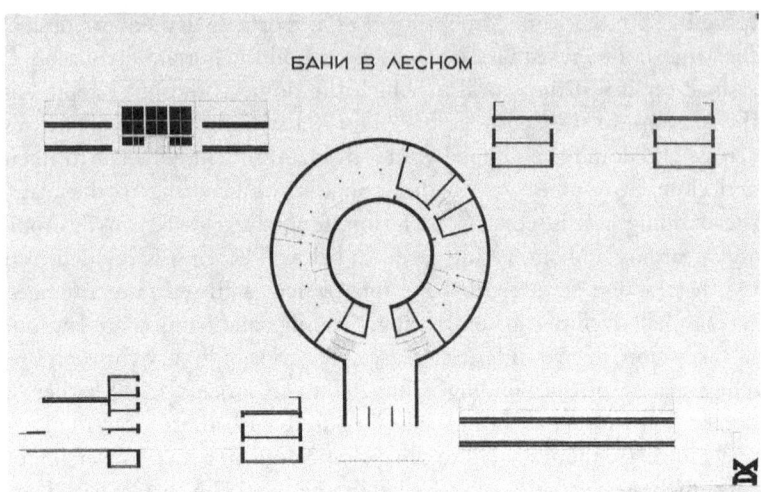

4.8 Alexander Nikolsky, project for a bathhouse, the design that was built in 1930.

"physculture," the development of which is an essential task of the Soviet government in the post-Revolutionary era, a task addressed not only by designers of *banyas* but also by "choreographers" of everyday life and production, such as Aleksey Gastev.

Nikolsky's round *banya* was never built according to the design of 1927. But the architect designed a scaled down and revised version that still exists (Figure 4.8). Between 1927 and 1930 NarKomStroi undertook the erection of a *banya* based on Nikolsky's scheme in a Leningrad suburb. The building was much smaller than the concept of the original. It could process only 2,400 citizens a day, and its diameter was only 21 metres – less than half of the size of the pool in the original plan – and the interior void is 9.5 metres in diameter. There was only one entrance to the building; it was not symmetrically divided for division of the sexes – men and women shared an entrance and occupied potentially separate floors. The perfect symmetry of the project is further lost when Nikolsky divides each floor into a smaller section for the first class of people and a bigger section for the second class. In the centre of the building is not a gigantic pool, a site of mass baptism, but a round well cut through the structure, open to the sky, as if articulating an uncertainty about what is in the centre of the communist universe.

The non-object

Regardless of the scaling down of Nikolsky's original project for the temple-like *banya* and the disappearance of the mechanical dome, El Lissitzky celebrated this project by publishing it in the November issue of 1931 of *SSSR na stroike* (*USSR in Construction*) (Figure 4.9). The journal, published between 1931 and 1941 in four languages (French, German, English, and Russian), was the most expensive and sophisticated Soviet propaganda publication at the time, and El Lissitsky was in charge of graphic design. In the photograph, whose horizon is at an extreme angle, the bathhouse is presented as seen from the air, with its edges cropped. This produces an unusual effect. The building seems to be both a three-dimensional object and a cropped surface, and thus seems to levitate in the air, rather than being firmly connected to the ground.

This angle and cropping of this photograph suggests that El Lissitsky was attracted to Nikolsky's project because the plan of his building was an abstract geometric shape. The photograph shows it both as a physical

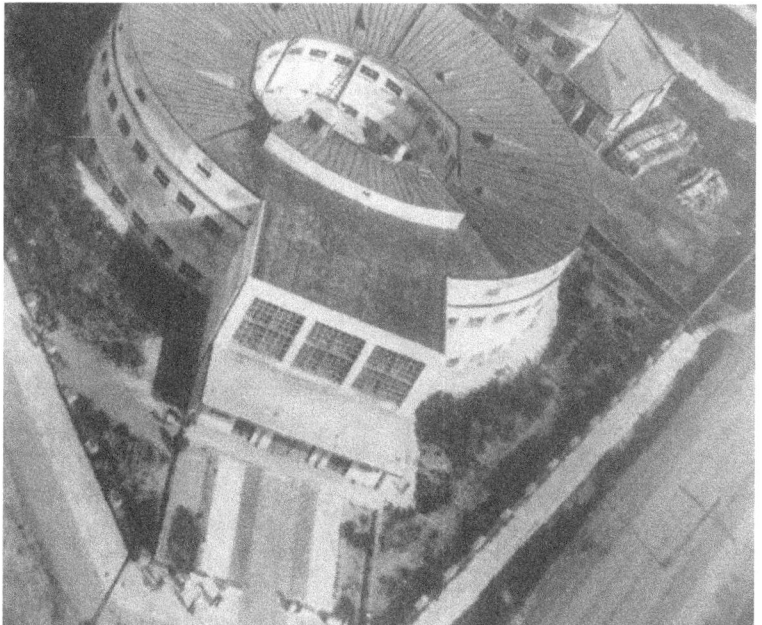

4.9 Nikolsky, "Round bathhouse," *USSR in Construction*, 1931.

object and a picture – an abstract surface. This makes sense since Nikolsky was a fellow suprematist. He was the only (trained) architect who joined the suprematist movement, spearheaded by El Lissitzky and Kazimir Malevich, whose members gathered around the Institute for Artistic Culture (INKhUK) in Leningrad after Malevich's move from Vitebsk in 1922.[21] The photograph in *USSR in Construction* resembles Malevich's early suprematist paintings, which were inspired by views of the city from above, from a perspective in which buildings were perceived as abstract shapes. Some of Malevich's paintings, such as "House Under Construction" of 1915 (Figure 4.10), present buildings as dynamic compositions of coloured rectangles. The "arkhitektons" of the early 1920s (Figure 4.11), which thread the boundary between abstract shapes and buildings, between models and sculptures, were intended to be inserted into the urban landscape to draw attention to the city's presence as both an assemblage of utilitarian structures and as an abstract geometric composition, to architecture's simultaneous existence as an object and a picture. In his manifesto of suprematism, Malevich insisted that there are "two types of creation": that which serves practical life and that of the "superconscious or subconscious mind," which deals with abstraction.[22] The arkhitektons introduced the production of the "superconscious mind" into architecture and urban life. The intent was to imbue urban life with a mystical dimension, to provoke awareness of "absolute, enduring values" beyond the "objective world" by defamiliarizing the environment, making it appear as if seen for the first time and presenting it as an assemblage of geometric surfaces – as pure form.[23]

The suprematists' formalist approach to painting, architecture, and the city is radically different from the Western functionalist rhetoric of a machine aesthetic in architecture in the 1920s and the 1930s. The most important aspect of the suprematist approach is that form was autonomous, and the partial independence of form from its practical purpose enables it to serve as a link between the everyday and the absolute. In the case of architecture and arkhitektons, abstract form introduced into the urban milieu connected abstract form, mystical ideas, and the urban environment.

The "feasible" universe

In Nikolsky's case, the mystical character of the *banya*, its status as a site of ritual, a world within a world, was closely tied to its graphic

4.10 Kazimir Malevich, *House under Construction*, 1915.

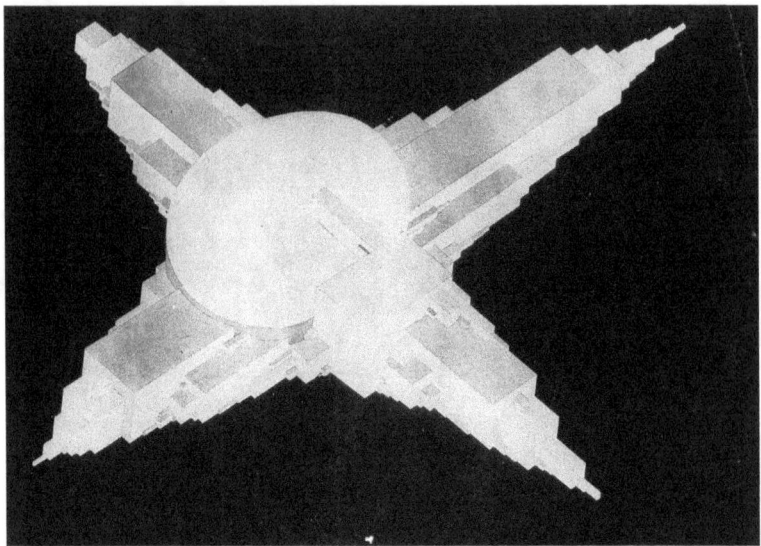

4.11 Ilya Chashnik, Suprematist Arkhitekton with Central Nucleus, 1928.

simplicity and perfect geometry, an abstraction of the world. The circle was the form of the absolute but also perfectly practical. Nikolsky's was a suprematist attempt to introduce elements of the universal, the sublime, into everyday activity. But it also belonged to the discourse on the most practical ways to operate a factory or, for that matter, any other socialist institution. The round plan was, indeed, around 1930 promoted as the universal solution to practical problems of many kinds of Soviet facilities. For example, in the June 1930 issue of the journal *Stroitelstvo Moskvy* (*Construction in Moscow*), dedicated to municipal construction, is an article on the "Standard design of a round building."[24] The circular plan, with different alterations, can be applied to a house, a school, an administrative building, a communal dining room, a kindergarten, or a workers' club. Another article, featured in the same issue and titled "Twelve bread factories," celebrates the modernization and mechanization of food production during the First Five-Year Plan.[25] The correspondent singles out Bread Factory No. 5, designed by Mrsakov, where all processes unfold on a circular plan. There are three concentric circles, connected with each other in the production process. The correspondent stresses that there are six new bread factories under construction in

The world in the bathhouse

Moscow, all based on a circle, in which "a great compactness" is achieved and the process of production flows seamlessly from the mixing of ingredients to delivery.

The ultimate achievement in blending pragmatism with mysticism, with presenting technology as sacred and the sacred as efficient, is to be seen in a project which evolved from Nikolsky's projects for Leningrad's public baths and for which he was an advisor: Anatoly Ladinsky's design for a round bathhouse in the Siberian city of Tyumen, which opened in 1931 (Figure 4.12). The project was published in the January 1932 issue of *Stroitelstvo Moskvy* (*Building in Moscow*) under the title, "When is the erection of structures without direct lighting feasible?"[26] The main topic discussed by the architect was the optical isolation of the building from its surroundings, and the fact that most of the washing and the steaming takes place in the dim space of the bath interior. Ladinsky presents the building as the most practical, most efficient version of the bathhouse ever invented. Most of the text is about Ladinsky's justification of the round shape as a practical design: the need to concentrate the infrastructure in the centre of the building and to place baths and saunas close to it, and the problems with placing showers next to exterior walls, which are then ruined by moisture and ice.

The process of bathing in this work of ultimate utility and practical genius is a passage through four connected round areas. Ladinsky's world of hygiene consists of four concentric zones: the saunas, showers, and lockers, with two corridors around them for access. They are arranged according to temperature. The heating shaft, 3 metres in diameter, is in the centre. It is surrounded by saunas, which are encircled by a band of showers. Cold dressing rooms and lockers are around the periphery of the building.

For Ladinsky, the bathhouse is not a place in which the citizen dwells. It is a place of movement, a choreographic instrument. The bather does not linger in the bathhouse, but spends five minutes undressing, forty minutes washing and steaming, and fifteen minutes dressing, and so accomplishes the task in an hour of constant activity and movement. The bathers follow a planned path, which prevents mixing of the dirty and the clean: they enter by a "dirty" staircase, take off their clothes, and put them in a two-sided locker. They proceed to the washing room and the sauna, then go into another "clean" hallway, approaching their locker from the other side, dresses, then exit the building through the other, "clean" staircase.

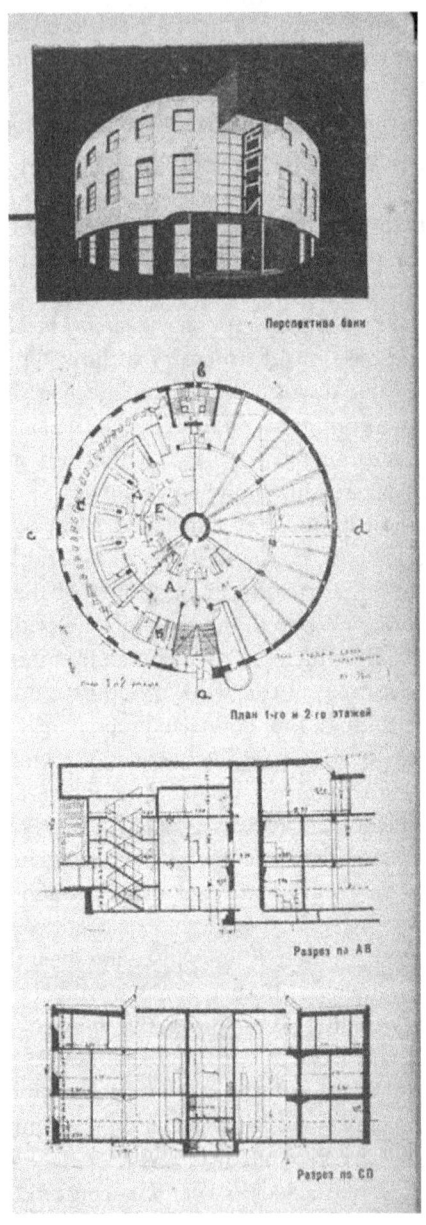

4.12 Anatoly Ladinsky, "Bath in Tyumen," *Stroitelstvo Moskvy*, 1932.

The world in the bathhouse 119

This journey of washing is akin to a ritual – the ritual in which bathers submit to the building-machine and the institution it embodies in a process of "purification." In this building the concept of a "sanitary conveyor" and the concept of the bathhouse-as-world converge. Ladinsky's and Nikolsky's schemes define the building as an ecosystem both physically and optically closed upon itself. This system is a "practical" engineered object, but also the site of purification and transformation rituals. While the layout of the bathhouse conserves energy, it is also a cosmological system. Nikolsky's designs were microcosmic – the building, referencing an Orthodox temple, represented the world. Ladinsky's design goes even further. Planned with progressively hotter layers organized around a burning core, it resembles a planet, or even the solar system (Figure 4.13). The ritual of self-care, marked by experiences of

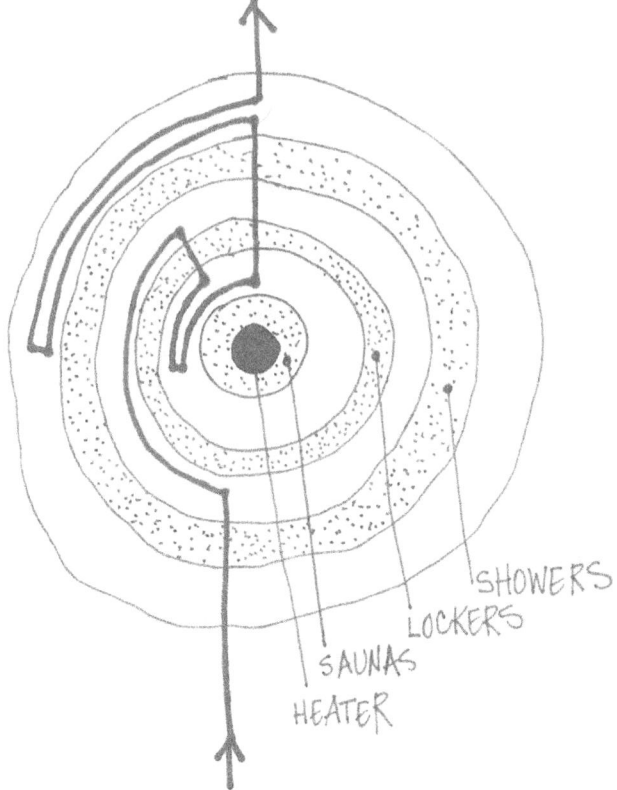

4.13 Bath in Tyumen, scheme of the bathing sequence.

heating and cooling, is the journey to the centre of the universe and back. And at the centre of this universe, in place of the sun, is a gigantic heater.

In conclusion, the *banya* of the 1930s was a site where the citizens could have their laundry done but also where they experience the frailty and ephemerality of the body, along with the ecstasies of collective immersion. The building type that captured the ethos of the First Five-Year Plan was based on a strange coupling of Taylorist rhetoric with mystical and metaphysical vision. *Banyas* were mechanical ecosystems made of bodies, substances, machines, and symbolic ecosystems, microcosms of the harmony and progress of the Soviet world. *Banya* projects of around 1930 embody a transition from a productivist to a representational architecture. The biomechanical stage and the operable home interior, discussed in previous chapters, articulate the idea that the physical environment, in the 1920s, is a site of production. Meyerhold's designs for the stage translated the idea of proletarians as working bodies in action; in the modern Soviet home, the worker was supposed to be physically "trained" to approach all of life as a type of work. Now the importance of how the building "works" gives way to the significance of what it represents. Through a ritual engagement with the building, the users learn to understand and appreciate this representation.

The aesthetics of the urban *banya* of the 1930s announce the advent of socialist realism as a system of representation. When discussed in architectural terms, socialist realism identified with neo-classicism, but is more broadly defined as the art of turning environments into microcosmic representations of the Soviet order in order to promote it as the paradigm of beauty, wealth, and harmony. In this sense, architecture advanced the myth of Soviet progress and prosperity, which informed social relations and served to reinforce relationships of power. But the process of "materializing" this myth, of translating it into built form, was marked not only by faith in the Soviet myth but also by a considerable dose of exuberance and eccentricity, an unchecked appetite for glamorizing the everyday through built form. The next chapter is about a similar appetite and the relationship between official myth and its execution in the quotidian environment. I will describe what can be termed a "minor genre" of socialist realism: the attempt of provincial housewives to personalize Stalinist rhetoric in their designs for homes and factory gardens published in a women's journal.

Notes

1 Mikhail Zoshchenko, "The Bathhouse," in *Scenes From the Bathhouse, and Other Stories of Communist Russia*, trans. Sidney Monas and ed. Marc Slonim (Ann Arbor: University of Michigan Press, 1962).
2 Ibid., 24.
3 Ivan Kudryakov, "Dvorets zdorovya" (Palace of health), *Kultura i byt*, no. 13 (1930): 67.
4 Ibid.
5 In 1928 N. I. Gundorov's Stalin Baths (*Stalinskie bani*) and S. V. Panin's Proletarian Baths (*Proletarskie bani*) in Moscow were completed. In 1930 *Kruglaya banya* (Round Bath) and *Gigant*, both designed by Alexander Nikolsky, were built in Leningrad. The *Gavanskie bani* were transformed into the *Sanpropusnik Vasileostrovskogo Raiona* (Sanitary Conveyer of the Vasileostrovsky District) in 1931, and the *Raznochinnye bani* were renovated in 1932. These reconstructions were designed by Alexander Gegello. Nikolay Demkov designed two standardized baths in Leningrad, on Ligovskaya and Stantsionnaya streets.
6 According to the surveys of *BanPrachProekt* (The State Agency for Designing Banyas and Laundries) in 1931, Moscow had a total of fifty-four baths for 2.75 million inhabitants (*Gossudarstvenny Arkhiv Russkoi Federatsii* (GARF), Fonds 314, Opis 1, Delo 5417, 1). Leningrad had fifty-five baths for around 2.75 million inhabitants, according to V. A. Rammo ("*Na poroge novogo bannogo stroitelstva*" (On the threshold of new bathhouse construction), *Voprosy kommunalnogo khoziaistva*, no. 1 (January 1931): 47. If some people bathed at home, according to the survey, one could approximate that a citizen took seventeen baths a year, which translates into 1.42 baths a month.
7 The procedure entailed steaming in an extremely hot steam room (*parilka*), being beaten with birch twigs (*veniki*) for circulation, and exposing oneself to cold water in tubs or showers or outside in snow in the countryside. This was a ritual of tempering the body, which produced extreme states and moods, with the final aim of strengthening the body and the spirit. Traditionally, exposure to extreme temperatures was of equal importance to washing. As described in H. Veber's *Zapiski Vebera o Petre Velikom* (quoted in I. A. Bogdanov, *Tri veka peterburgskoi bani* (*Three Centuries of the Petersburg Bath*). Saint Petersburg: Isskustvo-SPB, 2000, 42), the ritual would begin with heating the sauna until one could not stand on the floor of the room for fifteen seconds. Five or six men would enter the room, and their friend would close the sauna tightly. When they could hardly breathe, they would start yelling and he would let them out to get some fresh air. Then they would enter the sauna again and would repeat this until they

were completely red. Then they would jump into a river, or into snow in the winter, and stay in the river or snow covered up to their nose for several hours, "depending on what their medical condition would require, and they considered this method one of the main means of medical recovery."
8 N. A. Goldenberg, divizionyi vrach 25-I pekhotnoi divizii, *Banya dlya voisk i dlya narodnykh mass v gigienicheskom, sanitarnom, lechebnom i ekonomicheskom otnoshenii: kratkie vrachey ukazaniya dlya vrachei; dlya voyskovikh chastey, gorodskikh i zemskikh upravlenm; dlya shkol, fabrik, zavodov, i dr.* (N. A. Goldenberg, doctor of the 25th Infantry Division of the Russian Army, *The Bath for Armies and for Popular Masses – its Sanitary, Medical and Economical Aspects: Short Instructions for Doctors, for Military Units, for Municipal and District Governments; for Schools, Factories, Plants, etc.*) (St Petersburg: E. Evdokimov, 1898).
9 Ibid., 6.
10 Ibid., 2.
11 Ibid., 56.
12 Ibid., 9–10.
13 We can get a sense of what this looked like by following the case against the private trust *Stroitel* (Builder) in 1930, brought to light in the specialist Leningrad journal *Voprosy kommunalnogo khozaistva* (*Problems of Municipal Economy*) published by the Advertising Trust of the Section for Municipal Economy of the Leningrad District (*Reklamtrest Leningradskogo oblastnogo Otkomhoza*). In the July issue of 1930 (V. P. Ivanov, "*Istoriya chastnicheskogo Bannogo tresta*" (The history of the private bath trust): 62), the author explains that the trust rented seven baths from the Leningrad Regional Department of Municipal Economy (LGOKKH). According to the rulings of the Leningrad Regional Court of 1930 the agreements were annulled and the baths went back to the Bathhouse and Laundry Management (*Banno-Prachechnoe Khoziastvo*). The case against *Stroitel* was not a criminal but an ideological one. The renters were "unmasked." What the court discovered was that the trust was "capitalist in its essence" and that it only "worked in the guise of a workers' association."
14 "*Na pervoi oblastnoi konferentsii po sotsialisticheskomu pereustroistvu byta (17–20 marta)*" (At the first regional conference on the socialist reform of everyday life (March 17–20)), *Voprosy kommunalnogo khozyastva* (*Problems of Municipal Economy*, no. 3 (March 1930): 38.
15 "Social and communal laundries," *Voprosy kommunalnogo khozyaystva*, no. 2 3 (February March 1931). 60–69.
16 T. M. Semenova, "*Istoriya proektirovaniya pervogo petrogradskogo krematoriya*" (The history of designing the first Petrograd crematorium), in *Kraevedicheskie zapiski SPb—Issledovaniya i materialy*, no. 4 (1996): 236. Despite many

designs and building attempts of the 1920s and the 1930s, the first Leningrad crematorium was not actually built until 1972.
17 Bogdanov, *Tri veka peterburgskoi bani,* 142.
18 *"Ob usilenii rabot bo vyyavljeniyu i ispolzovaniu otkhodov v bannoprachechnom khoziaistve,"* GARF, Fonds 314, Opis 1, Delo 5320, 7–8.
19 Ibid., 8.
20 El Lissitzky, *Russia: An Architecture for World Revolution* (1930), trans. Eric Dluhosch (Cambridge: MIT Press, 1970), 27.
21 See Dimitrii Kozlov, "*Aleksandr Nikolskii i suprematisty* (Alexandr Nikolsky and the suprematists) in *Sbornik trudov fakulteta istorii iskusstv Evropeiskogo universiteta v Sankt-Peterburge (Journal of the School of History of Art of the European University in Saint Petersburg),* (2007): 98–114.
22 Kazimir Malevich, *The Non-Objective World: The Manifesto of Suprematism* (Mineola: Dover Publications, 2003), 16.
23 Ibid., 36.
24 *Stroitelstvo Moskvy,* no. 6 (June 1930): 15–16.
25 Ibid., 18–21.
26 Anatoly S. Ladinsky, "*Ratsionalizatsiya proektirovaniya tait v sebe ogromnye vozmozhnosti ekonomii: Kogda tselesoobrazna postroika zdanii bez pryamogo osveshcheniya?*" (The rationalization of design hides great potential for economizing: When is the construction of buildings without direct lighting purposeful?), *Stroitelstvo Moskvy,* no. 1 (Jan., 1932): 30.

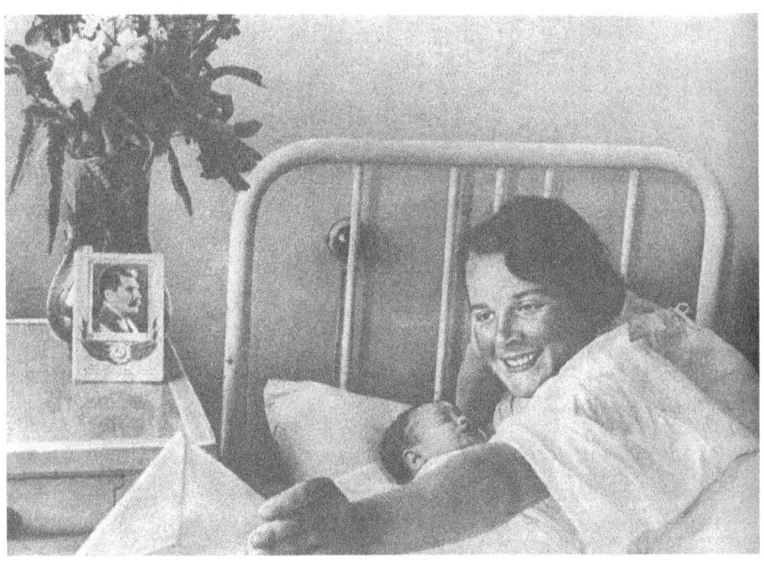

5.1 Young mother votes at the labour ward for the best friend of working women and children, comrade Stalin, *Obshchestvennitsa*, 1938.

5

Stalin and the housewife

The socially minded woman

A young mother lays in an iron bed, her head on her elbow and a smile on her face, the picture of a happy mother. She reaches across her newborn baby to hand the viewer an envelope (Figure 5.1). A framed photograph of Stalin rests on the bed stand, next to a bouquet of fresh flowers. The caption to this image explains that the woman is voting for the person in the photograph, who is her and the child's "best friend."

This is an image of a Soviet labour ward of 1938. Here, the father of the child is replaced by an image of the leader, which, not unlike an icon, figures as an object of veneration and source of protection. Indeed, Stalin's regime protected women. In the roaring Soviet 1920s the institution of marriage was challenged and described, as previously mentioned, as an official form of prostitution. Promiscuity was tolerated by men and women alike in the name of comradely love; abortion and divorce, previously stigmatized, were deemed acceptable. Accounts of this time reveal that women did not always appreciate this setup. A fascinating example is the letter of a young woman to a Soviet newspaper, which Sheila Fitzpatrick and Yuri Slezkin include in their collection of documents on women's lives in Russia. This woman describes her sexual escapades and writes to explain that she does not want to belong to the Communist Party because of how she was hurt by her lovers. The Party was to blame because it condoned the exploitation of women and the absence of male commitment to lovers and families in the name of "free love."[1] The conservative turn of the 1930s involved a backlash against the sexual revolution of the 1920s, in which new legislation was introduced, which banned abortion and made avoidance of paying child support very difficult.[2] The Soviet State took charge of protecting mother, children, and the traditional family. The photo on the bed stand is a symbol of this protection. But, unlike a wall portrait, for example, it is also a miniature, personalized version of the Soviet leader, of intimate dimensions and intimate character, like an icon.

This chapter is about a personalization of the Soviet political project and Stalinist propaganda in the publication in which the image of the mother voting for Stalin appeared: the journal *Obshchestvennitsa* (pictured in Figure 5.2), which translates as "the socially-minded woman." It came out between 1936 and 1941, and printed between 10,000 and 80,000 copies per year. It was the mouthpiece of a women's movement begun by those wives of engineers and technical specialists who had abandoned their occupations in order to accompany their husbands to remote parts of the country. Accordingly, its authors and audience consisted not of working women but of a particular class of Soviet housewives. Many of the engineers' wives were of "bourgeois origin," and social engagement for them was a way to cleanse them of this stigma. Through their "socially minded" activities and publications they were to become new, truly communist, women.

5.2 Women reading *Obshchestvennitsa* together, *Obshchestvennitsa*, 1938.

The editorship of *Obshchestvennitsa* cannot be firmly established, and appears to have been changed frequently, with different constellations of women in charge. The journal had an official editorial board only in the first year of publication. The board included Yevgenia Yezhova, the editor of the luxurious international propaganda publication *USSR in Construction* and the wife of the chief of NKVD (People's Commissariat of Internal Affairs), directly involved in the Purge. Among the editors was also Vera Schveister, the official of the People's Commissariat of Heavy Industry. By the end of 1937, no official editors are cited. After 1937, the journal may have been ghost-edited by the Commissariat of Heavy Industry, because the Commissariat was responsible for naming the movement of socially minded women.

The movement of "socially minded women," of which the journal was a mouthpiece, emerged in 1934. The story goes that it began with a horticultural intervention in a factory yard. In a metallurgical plant in Krasnouralsk, the wife of a station manager, a woman by the name of Surovsteva, created, in a dirty factory yard, an island of beauty and tranquillity – a square planting of flowerbeds. On his tour of the factory, the Commissar of Heavy Industry, Grigory Ordzhonikidze, was delighted when he noticed this intervention, and pronounced the woman "a pioneer of the movement of wives – *obshchestvennitsy*."[3] His own wife was soon to follow Surovtseva's example.[4]

What is immediately apparent is that "social mindedness" meant the inclination to embellish and beautify the industrial landscape, albeit with modest or makeshift means. "Social" expertise was, in the case of *obschestvennitsy*, aesthetic expertise. The movement is in many ways a continuation of women's activism from the 1920s, but this time its protagonists were not proletarian women but (mostly) housewives.[5] In addition, the activity of participants in this movement was to cultivate a sense for beauty, rather than to deal with practical issues, as the socially minded women of the 1920s did.

Activism as the pursuit of beauty

In the narratives of the 1920s, the activist is a proletarian man or woman. They discuss everyday problems, such as providing adequate nutrition for the family and balancing work duties and care for the household. They do not address problems of design and beauty. In contrast, the journal *Obshchestvennitsa* never acknowledges that life is hard. It

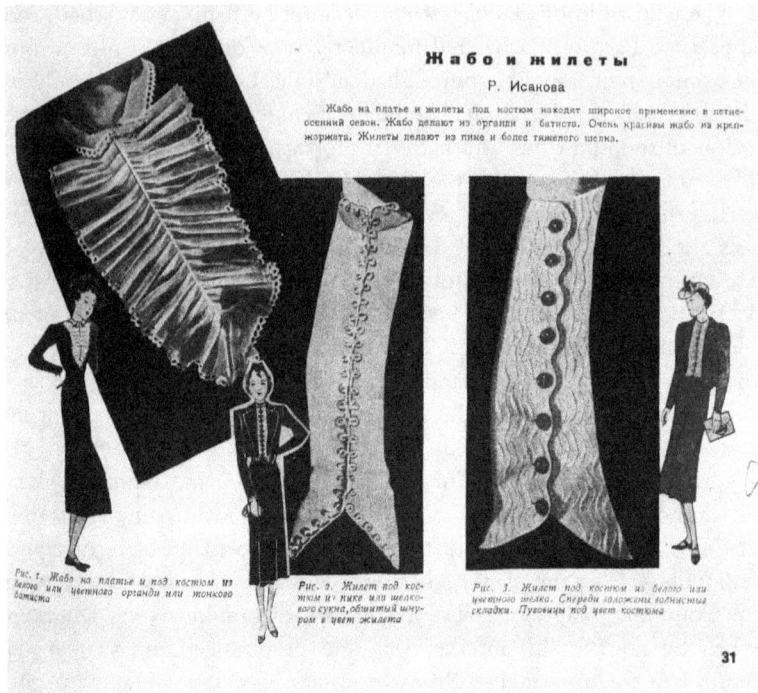

5.3 Jabot and jackets, *Obshchestvennitsa*, 1937.

resembles a Western women's magazine in that it is about the construction of the self through seemingly frivolous things. It provides advice on all aspects of femininity: trends in diets and fashion, such as the *jabot* and matching jackets (Figure 5.3), hallmarks of 1930s fashion; advertisements for face creams (Figure 5.4); images of the appropriate attire for tennis, skiing, and gymnastics; and instructions for exercise. The complete body of aesthetic expertise, which represented "social mindedness" in domains suitable for women, extended from the care of the self to the decoration of the home, including horticulture and the design of communal dining rooms, yards, and dormitories.

Communist beauty, as understood by the socially minded woman, began with the design of one's own body. And there was a template for it. The only colour spread in the history of the journal appears in the very first issue – a foldout reproduction of Rubens's *Holy Family* (Figure 5.5). The Soviet housewife was to be like the Virgin, not only in her symbolic capacity to conceive children with Stalin through immaculate

5.4 Ads for face creams "Flora" and "Onyx," *Obshchestvennitsa*, 1938.

conception, illustrated by the first image (Figure 5.1) in this chapter, but also in her plump appearance, which corresponded to the depiction of Mary in art.

To look like her counterpart in Rubens, the socially minded woman had to pay attention to cosmetics and nutrition. Care of the face and hair entailed elaborate rituals, illustrated by pictures of women applying various products. One of the authors of articles on hair, body, and skin was the director of the Moscow Institute of Cosmetics and Hygiene, who celebrates the quality and availability of cosmetic products created by the Soviet industry, such as the soap Detskoe for cleaning the face, the cooling creams Flora and Snezhinka, and the moisturizing creams Lanolinovy, Lotos, and Ogurechny for dry skin.[6]

5.5 Peter Paul Rubens. *Holy Family with the Basket*, 1616, reprinted in *Obshchestvennitsa*, 1936.

Living in the land of plenty

The director of the cosmetics and hygiene institute also stresses that proper nutrition is key to beauty. The wife-activist projected in *Obshchestvennitsa* did not try to solve the problem of hunger and scarcity of food, as the activists of the 1920s did, but was rather an avid consumer of supposedly abundant food. Her task was to eat well and feed her children well. The journal provides recipes and diets that scarcely manifest any attempt at frugality. Recipes are for pot-roasts and fruit salads. There are no diets for losing weight – the aim, in fact, is to get fat.

One diet, "How to Gain Weight," intended for teenagers and presumably self-respecting women, recommends sleeping nine to ten hours a day and eating cream, butter, condensed milk, margarine, lard, greasy pork and beef, fish and poultry, cakes, nuts, almonds, chocolate, honey, jam, and dried fruit.[7] Children were supposed to gain weight, too. A diet for small children recommends feeding them every couple of hours with milk, cookies, vitamin juice, ground apple, semolina kasha, pureed vegetables, sweet pudding, vegetable puree with liver or brains, eggs, fruit, pureed potato soup, and cutlet with carrot sauce. The aim was to make a child look like the Rubenesque Jesus.

An image in a 1937 issue of *Obshchestvennitsa* (Figure 5.6) features one such child. The plump baby is portrayed half naked, in socks and shoes but no shirt, the fat bulges of his torso clearly visible. The child sits on the ground among plants, next to a bucket presumably used to water them. His plump body is in fact part of a larger natural environment under the management of the socially minded woman. This environment in turn belonged to an imaginary, centrally managed Soviet ecosystem of bounty and fertility portrayed in socialist-realist science and popular culture. The world of plentiful food, well-nourished mothers and children, and advanced products for personal hygiene available to all was a complete fantasy. Poverty and hunger had not somehow disappeared in the 1930s. But the Soviet Union was nevertheless portrayed as a land of hyper-production and hyper-procreation. The movement of socially minded women emerged at the tail end of the Great Famine, when millions of people had very little food, and 5 million people in Ukraine starved to death – the result of forced collectivization and bad policies in the grain trade, which led to amassing grain supplies that were unavailable as food.[8] Although part of real life, these phenomena were not part of the picture of socialism, and their reality was erased from the doctored image of a socialist world. While a series of censuses, postponed and cancelled, would have shown a decrease in population and the number of births in this period,[9] socialism was portrayed as a universe of joy and plenty. In 1935 Stalin famously claimed that "life has become better, comrades, more joyous."[10] Enthusiastic official writing of this period proposed that in the Soviet Union, contrary to the conclusions of both Malthus and Marx, there is a potential for an infinite production of goods and an infinite growth of population, since the problem of surplus does not exist in the Soviet Union. As one commentator put it, "In our country, comrades, there is no danger of a surplus of population. There is also

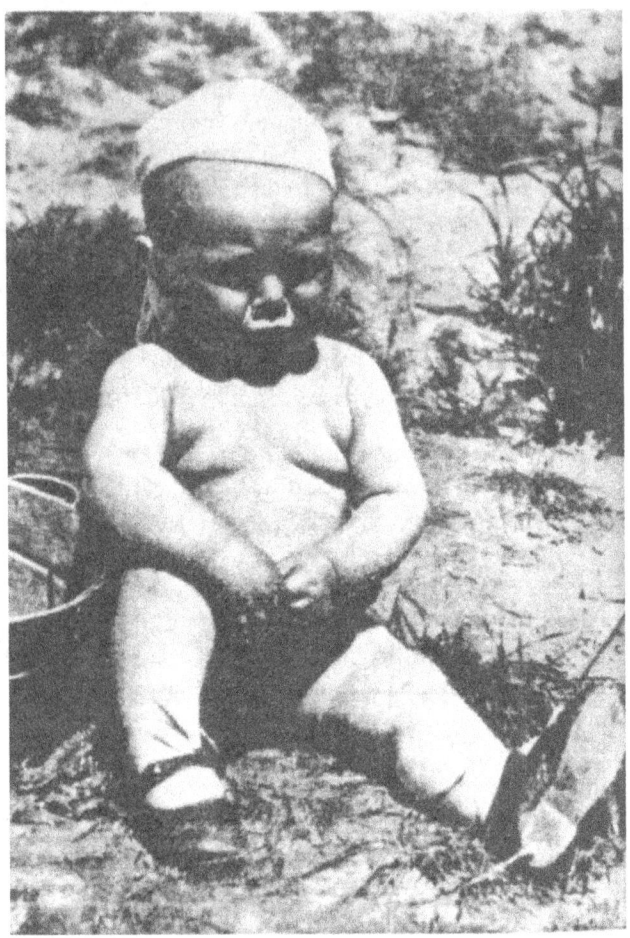

5.6 Untitled (child), in *Obshchestvennitsa*, 1937.

no danger of an overproduction of goods. The more people we have, the better for us, the more goods we have, the better."[11] Socialism was shaped as an image of infinite surplus: of people, of food, of commodities, and of joie de vivre.

The socially minded woman, whose primary identity is that of a mother rather than a worker, was meant to consume the imaginary surplus of goods and bring children to the good and joyous world of the late 1930s. This work of mothers of the communist collective is different to the motherhood of the 1920s. In the 1920s, experiments with Soviet motherhood entailed sharing bodily fluids – the communist offspring will become *bratya po moloku* (brothers in milk) when the State succeeds in collecting, mixing and redistributing mothers' milk for collective breastfeeding.[12] This common, nurturing Soviet mother, to which all children would attach and together form a collective, never developed because the huge project, while practical, was difficult to execute. In *Obshchestvennitsa*, children do not share milk, but rather a collective father. Numerous photographs in *Obshchestvennitsa* portray a mother holding a baby without a father present. The message is that, no matter what her station in life, the socialist woman does not need a husband for childrearing; she does not include him in such matters. Giving birth, too, takes place in his absence. Childrearing is the task of the socially minded women's collective, performed under the supervision of the collective father, Stalin. This absence of the biological father, and the induction of Stalin as the spiritual father of all, as the image of the Stalinist labour ward (Figure 5.1), implies "abstract" procreation, by which the mother passes the love of Stalin, the spirit of socialism, to the child. Organizing collective breastfeeding was difficult, but the project of creating a collective father was comparatively easy, since this father played a "spiritual" role in procreation. It was enough that he only appeared as an image, a representation, as in the photograph on the bedside table.

Socialism now was not a matter of organization and production, but of representation. In his *Political Economy of Socialist Realism*, Evgeny Dobrenko explains that socialist realism in the 1930s included not only monumental painting, novels, and classicist architecture, but also other projects describing and promoting socialism.[13] Agricultural theory, advertising, bureaucratic proclamations, pop culture, exhibitions – all were part of a cultural landscape of Stalinism, and participated in creating a glossy, seductive version of socialism. Socialist realism was a broad enterprise to make socialism real. Not only was an image of the society presented that was a mirage intended to dazzle the populace, but socialist realism defined political and economic interactions.

The question is how the movement of socially minded women and their publication, if we consider it a minor genre of socialist realism, related to its major forms. Which identities did this movement articulate? How did these identities fit into the Stalinist project of the 1930s? Let us start with the most paradigmatic example of socialist realism: the genre of monumental painting, as exemplified by Arkady Plastov's *Feast*

5.7 Arkady Plastov, *Feast on a Collective Farm*, 1937.

on a Collective Farm (Figure 5.7). The painting presents a scene of collective cornucopia and establishes the collective feast as a comprehensive metaphor for the society of plenty. In the background of the painting, a red banner with Stalin's words "life has become more joyous" hangs beneath his portrait. The socialist realist text is thus connected to the socialist realist image; the painting makes Stalin's words come to life by translating them into a scene in which peasants consume the abundance created by their hard work. The tables are loaded with food similar to that prescribed in the diet for socially minded women: dairy products, cakes, pies, fruit, wine, meat. The heaps of peaches, eggs, and bread in the foreground mirror the densely piled group of people in the background, forming a pyramidal composition framing a celebratory crowd. It is as if people and food can endlessly multiply. Such a fertile and prolific world, a realm of biological plenty bathed in the gentle autumn sun and painted in bright colours, stands in for all the supposedly glorious achievements of the Second Five-Year Plan.

Wall paint and potted plants: a minor genre of socialist realism

Socially minded women (*obshchestvennitsy*), according to their journal, mirrored socialist realist painting through their own aesthetic creations.

The study and interpretation of Rubens was, incidentally, identified as a prerequisite for socialist realism since its inception in 1932. In the words of Ivan Gronsky, Chairman of the Organizing Committee of the USSR Writers, who proposed the term "socialist realism," this aesthetic orientation was "Rembrandt, Rubens and Repin put at the service of the working class."[14] As socially minded women put Rubens in the service of their aesthetic education, they were also looking at Soviet art painted, like classical art, in "a correct and literate manner."[15] But the choice of painting for embellishing the interior as well as educating a child's taste was not monumental, large-scale painting like Plastov's, but a minor genre perceived appropriate as the model for design interventions by women: the still life. In one of the photographs in the journal, a still life hangs above a cabinet in a nursery, an interior design coordinated with the everyday world depicted in the painting (Figure 5.8). On the cabinet are fabric, bowls, and a bulbous vase, reflecting the shape and highlights of the fruit and the colour and texture of the cloth in the painting.

The resonance between the painting and interior decoration underscores the painterly nature of women's expertise. While the design of the built environment was the purview of the professional male architect, a peculiar body of expertise emerges as the "feminine" realm of design: competence in selecting, matching, and applying colour. The woman, according to the journal, should "take advantage of the artistic role of the wall itself, as a fixed background in the interior."[16] The choice of wall finish was "a mass art in the full meaning of the word; in this colossal mass creation the woman has an active role as mistress and organizer of the home."[17] The treatment of the home as mass creation involved, for example, the following interventions in a nursery: "painting the walls, choosing electrical fittings, furniture, curtains, little paintings, colour for toys and even the colour of the caretaker's dress."[18]

One article, "The interior – its architecture and lighting design," regards the interior entirely as a painterly work. The reader of the journal should consider "the artistic aspects of painting the interior" and "pay attention to the advice of the artist and the architect and study the best models of interior design of buildings similar in type."[19] A socially minded woman should have the know-how of an artist and the expertise to reflect on coefficients for natural and artificial lighting. She should also reflect on the properties of objects outside. For example, trees outside the window create a green reflection in the room, and the

5.8 Side cabinet (buffet) in a nursery, *Obshchestvennitsa*, 1936.

walls should therefore be painted a light yellow colour. As design experts, women should also be able to differentiate between achromatic and chromatic colours, and to know when to use light and heavy tints. A separate body of knowledge was understanding the relationship between the properties of an object's surface that reflect its makeup – *faktura* – and properties of colour. The article provides instructions for using different colours for different geographic locations – cold tints in the south and warm tints in the north.

Practising the "mass art" of colour coordination that was the female domain required the acquisition of a considerable body of knowledge, which involved psychology and rules of perception. An article on nursery design, "Proportion, form, colour," explains that the woman should master "the laws of physics, physiology, physiological optics, colour science, history of art and pedagogy," and the possession of this knowledge prevents the woman from relying only on her taste, empowering her to develop an aesthetic sense that is scientifically grounded.[20] Physio-psychological expertise, according to another article, enables women "not to tire the eye and the psyche, not to disturb the physiological and the psychological balance of the organism, as the eye transfers the irritation from the retinal membrane to the brain."[21]

The word for colour, that main object of feminine knowledge, in the journal is *tsvet*. But this word also means flower. This homonymity plays a peculiar role in the aesthetic discourse in *Obshchestvennitsa*, for the second most important body of expertise, after colour, is expertise on flowers – horticultural know-how. The understanding of *tsvety*, or flowers, entailed the understanding of *tsvety*, or colours, and vice versa. Just as the founder of the movement, Surovtseva, did in the factory, the socially minded woman practised her social mindedness and motherly nature by "carefully and lovingly looking after young plantings," in the same way she looked after her children.[22] The emergence of *obshchestvennitsy* as a mass movement and the 1930s femininity it represented was epitomized in the creation of vegetal ornament. This ornament ranged from small potted plants to large-scale public installations for major holidays. The attention given to this topic is at its most intense in the journal in 1937. A journalist by the name of Sushkin wrote extensively about the "awakening of life" in nature after winter spent in a 12-inch pot.[23] For the plant to grow, the home had to be kept very warm during winter, which was not a problem: the Soviet Union was, purportedly, a land of wealth and prosperity.

According to Sushkin, there are two important areas of expertise required for planting and the design of horticultural arrangements. One is the understanding of different kinds of plants and the care they need. He writes about bulbous and tuberose plants, about shrubs and grassy perennials. He gives instructions about the choice of specimens of bulbs and branches, storage, light exposure, and watering. He complements practical with aesthetic instruction. In his article "The design of plantings," Sushkin writes that "to plant greenery one needs to know how to group trees, shrubs, and flowers so that they create a pleasant combination of forms and colours during the entire period of their growth from the early spring to late fall."[24] The socially minded woman was to master the proper arrangement of plants and those species that create a good composition. For instance, according to Sushkin, a good composition would be a centralized one of American dahlias surrounded by dark pygmy dahlias planted at a distance of 15 to 20 centimetres from the centre. Flowerbeds yield the most interesting compositions, as they can be planted in a round, oval, ellipsoid, square, rhomboid, polygonal, or star-shaped form. The purpose of all groupings of trees, shrubs, and flowers was the creation of flower "drawings, in tones and half-tones."[25] Slogans and portraits of leaders should be executed in the medium of plants. Flowerbeds can also be abstract art, made of one colour, with a thin border of another colour. Or plants can be grouped in concentric circles, where the tallest and the brightest plants are planted in the middle, and the height of plants and their brightness decreases towards the end. The wife-activist has the entire spectrum of colours available for the execution of her creations.

In winter the "awakening of nature" is a small-scale, domestic project. In spring it becomes an urban project and, as a collective public exercise, a crucial part of socialist festivities. In the article "Flowers and greenery in the celebrations of the first of May" of 1937, Sushkin explains that International Labour Day must be "beautiful and colourful"; the main means of its aesthetic articulation is the cultivation of special greenery.[26] A specific project was making "green posters" with portraits of leaders and revolutionary slogans. They can be produced, writes Sushkin, in a very sophisticated manner, by growing sprouts over several days in some sort of textile, to create a grassy fabric, and then decorating it with flowers to form letters and images. The celebration of spring involved decorating windowsills, balconies, and facades with garlands and window plantings. For celebrating International Labour Day, women could also bring the plants they have grown in the tropical warmth of their home, such as palms and ficus trees, to their windows and balconies. Sushkin says that the production of horticultural architectural ornament has "ceased to be luxury, but is a necessity in the lives of the working class."[27]

Despite Sushkin's grandiose plans for women's horticulture, the actual projects by wife-activists shown in the journal are very modest. In one,

5.9 Fountain in the mechanical department of a train depot, *Obshchestvennitsa*, 1938.

the "fountain in the mechanical department of a train depot," a group of activists gather around a fountain within a pool with a dozen little pots arranged on the pool's edge (Figure 5.9). A working woman, her dress differentiating her from the group of women-activists, operates machinery in the background, indicating that the design work of *obshchestvennitsy* complements the woman's factory work. This labour of design also manifested itself in the project of "creating a flower garden in front of the passenger platform" of a train station (Figure 5.10). Here, in a photograph carefully framed by an overhead railway bridge, *obshchestvennitsy* crouch with their hands in or on the earth or stand holding a watering can and a gardening implement, nurturing a round garden that looks unremarkable, in black and white at least.

Fabricating the beautiful world

When we read about how women were, in practical terms, meant to apply their expertise on *tsvet*, photographs show real palm and ficus trees but the little gardens are not particularly luscious. It would be difficult to say that these pictures complement the ideology of abundance and fertility offered by state officials and presented visually in socialist realist paintings such as Plastov's *Feast*. They betray a lack of precise congruity between the rhetoric of surplus and the means that

5.10 Wife-activists of the Debaltsev station creating a flower garden in front of the passenger platform, *Obshchestvennitsa*, 1937.

women could employ to materialize this rhetoric in their interventions. We can also get a glimpse of the actual modesty of the means *obshchestvennisty* had at their disposal from articles published in the journal about how to make household objects at home, which implies that there is no abundance of mass produced goods. One article provides instruction on how to sew a spherical lampshade, suspended from the ceiling (*plafon*) in nurseries and bedrooms, out of coloured silk scraps.[28] The woman has to understand the proper sequence of colours: blue, pink, yellow, green, red, violet, white, pink, green, orange, cream. She also has to know how to mix powder paints and dissolve them in water, and then know how to boil silk in the dye to produce these colours.

Socially minded women were thus not only the designers of the communist home and garden but also their makers. They were expected not only to understand the physio-psychological properties of colour and be experts in the aesthetic impact of the wall, but also to paint the wall themselves. In an article called "Apartment renovation," the authors write that it is expensive to involve trade organizations, so the housewives should step in and organize "independent women's brigades," or groups of at least two people, and undertake the "rejuvenation of the environment" themselves.[29] The entire "renovation" consists of repainting the walls, and readers are given detailed instructions: how to remove existing colour, cover cracks, prime the walls, apply oil paint. The author provides exact proportions for making paint from pigment, chalk and paste for blue, yellow, green, red, and brown tints.

Then there is the *remont* (reconstruction and renovation) of communal spaces. Images in the journal present dance halls, collective dining rooms, and offices "beautified" by the socially minded woman. Just like the makeover projects of today, these are presented with "before" and "after" photographs.

In the "before" image (Figure 5.11), a group of workers and a couple of cooks gather around a meal served on a plain wooden table. A window with heavy dark drapes illuminates the meal and a bare light bulb dimly reveals rows of tables fitted with long benches. In the "after" image (Figure 5.12), the room is transformed: smaller tables are surrounded by four chairs; tablecloths, lampshades, and identical water tumblers rest on each table; sheer curtains are drawn to one side of the windows. The "before" and "after" photographs are not shot from the

5.11 "Before" image of a factory dining hall, *Obshchestvennitsa*, 1938.

5.12 "After" image of a factory dining hall, *Obshchestvennitsa*, 1938.

same angle, and show opposite sides of the room. It is as if the world "before" and the world "after" coexist in the same space, one on the left and the other on the right side of the room. The room with the wooden benches is the existing factory environment complete with its hard-working, hungry inhabitants, and the room with white tablecloths is a feminine version of this environment, fresh and ready for the inhabitants who have not yet arrived – the world of the joyous future.

The transformation that they produce makes the best of the modest resources available, but it is not a fundamental transformation of the material environment. The women-activists behind the transformation were complete amateurs situated on the margins not only of the design profession, but also of the provincial factory collective. However, unlike the major works of socialist realism, which depict and represent reality, the work of socially minded women translates representation into reality – into the concrete physical environment in which the workers live. In monumental painting, peasants consume an abundance of fruit and meat in soft autumn sunshine. Housewives try, as much as their means and experience allow, to bring this picture into life, acting as designers to colour-coordinate interiors with fruit in still life paintings and to paint walls so that the brightness of their colours expresses the radiant nature of socialist future. They decorate dining rooms with new furniture, carafes, and tablecloths so as to create the appropriate environment for consuming the cornucopia to be produced by Soviet industry.

If we return to Dobrenko's thesis about the "political economy of socialist realism" and assess the role in that economy played by the *obshchestvennitsy*, we find that their opus is located at a crucial point in the system. As Dobrenko writes, the economy of socialist realism mirrors the scheme of capitalist economy in its own characteristic way. In a capitalist economy, real experience is translated into abstraction and then back to reality – goods are exchanged for money and, subsequently, money is used to buy goods. In the economy of socialist realism, reality turns into a representation of reality which then starts shaping the lived and the real. Representation of socialism is the main currency of symbolic and economic exchange. Identities, status, economic relationships, and social values are tied to this currency, in a similar fashion to how they are tied to money in capitalism. By referencing the socialist realist imaginary and narratives, *obshchestvennitsy* integrate themselves into the Soviet economic and symbolic system and turn from suspect bourgeois wives into new socialist women. Their "social mindedness" is the acceptance of socialist realist representation, and in this case the Soviet reality of socialism is depicted as a world of bounty and fertility.

But they do more than that. Their adoption of socialist ideas for the sake of personal "cleansing" and social acceptance is but a true "buying into" of the Soviet representational system. The act of "renovating" provincial realities according to the socialist realist template is an enterprise that involves actual and enthusiastic attempts to transform the material environment, or at least some evolved ideas of what the world is supposed to look like "after" their beautification of the grim environment, "after" the peculiar implementation of the socialist political programme in spaces of the everyday by means of design. The socialist realist representation is rendered concrete, rendered real. In the context of *remont*, artificiality is a desirable condition. The home, the body, the factory yard are not only real physical environments. Their value stems from the fact that they are artefacts corresponding to other artefacts, such as the socialist realist painting, the plump Madonna, advertisements, etc. The pictures "before" and "after" actually stress that *obshchestvennitsy*, like true socialist activists, have the power to transform life according to a *design*. As such, their activity is a small-scale version of socialist construction as a total and totalitarian social project.

Housewives' desire to "renovate" the world, to make it as beautiful and joyous as the socialist realist template is not merely an act of masking reality. Despite the enthusiasm, their projects remain shabby; their scale is pitiful. They reveal the actual poverty and the discord between imagined socialist glory and dismal reality rather than creating some kind of an alternative, elevated existence. But this ardent attempt to personalize the Stalinist picture of the world, to introduce socialist realist aesthetic into the most intimate environment, might indicate something important. It is possible that socialist realist art and architecture were not merely meant to mask this reality but to compensate for it, to transcend it, to invent spaces in which dignity can exist and to find dignity in their power to transform the world around them, albeit incompletely and with makeshift means.

Defending the *gesamtkunswerk* with their lives

The ideally "renovated" environment created by the socially minded woman is a total work of art, a *gesamtkunstwerk,* belonging to a larger *gesamtkunstwerk,* that of the Soviet society. "Life is becoming better," "life is becoming joyous," reads the narrative, because it is turning into a comprehensive work of art which encompasses all of existence and because it demonstrates the power of the Party to "renovate" the world. And, as Stalin's notorious sentence implies, this power is based both on political and aesthetic expertise.

By talking about Stalinist economy as representational, Dobrenko suggests that the political system of the 1930s is an aesthetic project. This idea is even more explicit from Boris Groys, who claims, in *The Total Art of Stalinism,*[30] that the oppressive 1930s regime was, in its totalitarian dimension, in many ways an extension of the avant-garde project dedicated to bringing art to life, to using aesthetic practice to transform all of existence. And that the desire to transform the totality of existence and forge a new human being is what aligned artists of the 1920s so closely with the Bolshevik regime. In previous chapters, we have seen that ideas about the New Man, over the course of Soviet history, are closely linked to the cosmic and celestial imaginary, a universal totality. This was true in the case of what I termed "productivist" projects of the 1920s, which involved ideas such as harmonizing the rhythms of labour with those of the universe, for example, or creating buildings as microcosms meant to reflect and refract the total order of things. In the 1930s the regime was driven by an ambition to control almost all aspects of life and all the subjects, and it used art – representations of reality – to achieve that.

This representational system was so comprehensive that it could subsume contradicting experiences of fear, anguish, and uncertainty within the picture of a joyous society. The case of socially minded women demonstrates this. Their project is consistent even in the paradoxical situation where death and devastation creep into the world of infinite bounty, fertility, and joy. Scattered among the photographs of well-ordered environments – dresses, cosmetic products, fat babies, landscapes of flowerbeds – are images of women in gas masks. A government representative gives a lesson in chemical warfare (Figures 5.13). Women learn to drive in gas masks, and go on hikes in gas masks (Figure 5.14). The esprit de corps created through the quest of social mindedness and group identity is also a military esprit de corps, and the femininity of the well-kept visage, with silken hair and curvaceous body, has its double in the figure of the female soldier, the femininity of the apocalypse.

At a certain point in their subscription to *Obshchestvennitsa*, the reader learns that the main point of socialist motherhood, of the art of creating

5.13 Civil defence class, *Obshchestvennitsa*, 1937.

5.14 Driving classes wearing gas masks, *Obshchestvennitsa*, 1937.

a well-fed and strong child, is to sacrifice him to the socialist cause, similar to how the Virgin sacrifices her son for humankind. A poem titled "Mirror," published in 1938, on the eve of the Second World War, identifies the relationship of a child's socialist identity with his body and the bounty of nature:

> I come to the mirror
>
> I look at myself in it
>
> I move away, I move closer
>
> I see the same thing—
>
> A boy walking around all day
>
> Pale, like a shadow.
>
> I walk around sad, because I am not putting on weight.
>
> If I am weak and skinny,
>
> How will they take me into the army?
>
> How will I go to training?
>
> I will not be able to lift up the rifle.

I will not be able to get on the horse.

They will not take me!

One must be healthy,

One must be ready for defence,

Because everyone has to be

The defence of the country.

So I decided to get better

Started to force myself to eat:

I ate pea *kissel*,

Milk and *vermishel* [vermicelli]

Ham and sour milk,

Jam and buckwheat porridge,

Kulyebyaka and omelette …

Am I gaining weight or not?

I get to the mirror,

I look at myself in it.

I move away, I move closer

I see the same thing:

A boy walking around all day

Pale, like a shadow.

How will I get recruited?

I started eating more and more,

I ate everything

All that is sour, all that is sweet,

All that I don't like,

Just so that I would get fatter.

I tried to get better,

Started exercising.

I went each morning to drills,

Waking up all by myself.

Time passed unnoticeably

And three weeks went by.

I get to the mirror,

I look at myself in it.

I move away, I get closer,

But now I already see

There is a warrior in the mirror.

Well, I did not try for nothing.

I will go to training,

I will easily lift a rifle.

I will deftly get on the horse—

They will take me into the army![31]

Socially minded wives participated in the total project of socialist realism by linking representation to reality, by "renovating" reality to fit the picture. They were also ready to defend this renovated reality in the most concrete sense, by giving their own lives and the lives of their children for it. One image in the journal features "activists" in an oil field in Baku, in the Azerbaijan Soviet Socialist Republic, apparently "finishing their training mission," according to the caption (Figure 5.15). Nine women march in military formation, equipped with "protective" garb, prepared to defend the oil rigs looming in the background, the natural source of socialism's wealth and plenty. The lush garden is, in this image, replaced with a desert, presumably on the outskirts of the housewives' carefully planted oasis. Beyond the fragile feminine landscape of joy and wellbeing most often explored in the journal looms the threat of death, and of danger – danger to the world of housewives' creation. The danger does not come from the internal enemies of the Revolution – those persecuted in the Great Terror, for example – but from an external enemy ready to seize the resources necessary for

5.15 Activists of the oil plant in the name of Kaganovich (in Baku) finishing their training mission in gas masks. *Obshchestvennitsa*, 1937.

producing socialist cornucopia. The presence of this danger makes the fragile world of socialist beauty even more precious. And the enthusiastic effort to create socialist beauty in turn fuels the zeal for military action. The depiction of imminent danger and destruction, the call for military readiness, is woven into the partially absurd – yet sublime – effort of housewives to transcend reality and assume the role of active designers of socialism. It launches their aspirations from the realm of homes and gardens to the distant deserts of the Middle East, transforming the minor artists of socialist realism into its ardent soldiers. In the construction of the ideal socialist society, creating a biological surplus, a wealth of people, means creating not just citizens who will enjoy the riches of a supposedly developed industrial society, but a population that can itself be consumed. The housewives themselves are getting ready to fall for their country. And their country is the imago they participated in creating and transforming into reality.

Matters of life and death, and the willingness to sacrifice oneself to the socialist cause, depended on how much one believed in a fantastic representation of the social system, which described it not in ethical or political terms but in aesthetic terms – as a beautiful and harmonious world. One of the most totalizing, and totalitarian, projects in modern history was an art project and, in that sense, skin deep. The fact that the contributors to *Obshchestvennitsa* understood their "social mindedness" as essentially a cosmetic expertise – the knowledge of colour and ornament applied to one's body, home, and nature at large – indicates that the participants in this project took superficiality seriously. Being an ideal Soviet subject in the 1930s meant understanding its aesthetic codes, knowing how to appreciate the *gesamtkunstwerk* of socialism. Knowing how to create and recreate this total work of art and mastering its rules ensured participation in the Stalinist political project.

The next chapter continues to explore this notion further, with a project on an entirely different scale: the Moscow Metro, the grandest public work of the 1930s, incredibly opulent, expensive, and monumental. However, those who created this socialist realist masterpiece – the Metro construction workers – were similar to housewives in that they understood the act of building "beautiful" environments to be an act of transforming themselves into socially minded subjects. The project they participated in was, despite its vast scale, essentially cosmetic, based on an expertise applied to the texture, colour, and luminosity of surfaces. In this case, however, this kind of aesthetic expertise will, for the Party and the ordinary citizens alike, become the essence of understanding, describing, and experiencing socialist progress. It will demonstrate the congruence between "personalized" socialist realist projects made with makeshift means, and the colossal all-Soviet masterpiece, which both defined the politically conscious subject as a connoisseur of socialist beauty.

Notes

1 See Paraskeva Ivanova, "Why I Do Not Belong in the Party," originally published in L. Sosnovsky, ed. *Bolnye voprosy (zhenshchina, semya i deti) (Painful Issues (Woman, Family and Children))* (Leningrad: Priboy, 1926), reprinted in abridged form in Sheila Fitzpatrick and Yuri Slezkine, eds, *In the Shadow of the Revolution: Life Stories of Russian Women from 1917 to the Second World War* (Princeton: Princeton University Press, 2000), 213–218.
2 The decree on the family of 27 June 1936 brought by the Central executive committee of the Soviet of People's Commissar's of SSSR instituted a two-year jail sentence for performing abortion and made divorce very difficult, since the parties had to pay fines and have the divorce recorded in their passports. See *O zapresheny abortov; uvelichelny materiyalnoy pomoshchi rozhenitsam, ustanovlenny gosudarstvennoy pomoshchi mnogosemeynym, rashireny seti rodylnikh domov, detskikh yasley i detskikh sadov, usileny ugolovnogo nakazaiya za neplatezh alimentov i o nekotorykh izmeneniyakh v zakonodatelstve o razvodakh*. (On the Ban of Abortion, the Increase in Material Aid to Women in Childbirth, the Institution of Government Aid to Families with Many Children, the Expansion of the Network of Childbirth Facilities, Nurseries and Kindergardens, the Increase of Criminal Punishment for Non-Payment of Child Support and some Alteration in Divorce Legislation).
3 Rebecca Balmas-Neary, "Flowers and Metal: The Soviet 'Wife-Activists' Movement' and Stalin-Era Culture and Society 1934–1941" (PhD diss., Columbia University, 2002), 1.
4 Ordzhonikidze's wife was a member of the Industrial Commanders' Wives Movement, which appeared in 1935 in the Kirov iron and steel plant in Makeevka in the Donbass coalfield, one of the largest steel plants in the world, with 20,000 workers. Ordzhonikidze was a patron of this plant and a close friend of its director Gvakhariya. See Francesco Benvenutti, "Industry and purge in the Donbass 1936–1937," *Europe-Asia Studies*, 45, no. 1 (1993): 68–69.
5 In "Flowers and Metal," Balmas-Neary analyses the roles of the wife-activist as a spouse, mother, and public figure. While the goals of activism were often meant to be pursued in the intimacy of the domestic interior, the movement was not, Balmas-Neary argues, a total Stalinist regression towards traditional family values, but the continuation of women's activism from the 1920s in a completely different form and under new circumstances. Balmas-Neary also argues that the wife-activist movement, however apparently conservative, did not, in fact, entail the existence of a stable gender system, since the role of a spouse, loyal to her husband, and the role of a public figure, loyal to the common cause, were in most cases difficult to reconcile.

6 In her book *The Soviet Dream: World of Retail Trade and Consumption in the 1930s* (London: Palgrave Macmillan, 2008), Amy Randall elaborates on the rise of consumer culture and advertising of commodities in the Soviet Union of the 1930s. Old revolutionary ideals of asceticism were abandoned, and new Soviet citizens were defined not only as producers, but also as consumers. Rationing, though it could not be abandoned until the mid-1930s, was condemned as early as 1931, and the ideal was to create an efficient and comfortable store, without queues, in which the citizen could buy what he or she wished. Soviet industry was incapable of meeting both this ideal and actual consumer needs but, nevertheless, modern retail stores became part of Soviet modern utopia together with technological achievements. Women were particularly targeted as subjects of new, enlightened, Soviet consumption, and were supposed to develop "Soviet taste."

7 V. Mendelson, "Kak popolnet'" (How to gain weight), *Obshchestvennitsa*, no. 16 (1937): 30–31.

8 R. W. Davies, M. B. Tauger, and S. G. Wheatcroft, "Stalin, grain stocks, and the famine of 1932–1933," *Slavic Review*, 54, no. 3 (1995): 651.

9 The census planned for 1935 was postponed until 1936, to be finally held on 7 January 1937. When the Statistical Commission found that, instead of 180 million people as Stalin hoped, or the minimum estimate of 170 million, the population of the Soviet Union was only 162 million, chief statistical professionals were arrested and imprisoned, the census was proclaimed invalid and postponed until 1939, when the numbers were grossly inflated.

10 Iosif Visaroionivich Stalin, "Speech at the First-Union Conference of Stakhanovites, November 17, 1935," in J. V. Stalin, *Problems of Leninism* (Peking: Foreign Language Press, 1976), 785.

11 Andrey Andreevich Andreev, "Kommunisticheskoe vospitanie molodezhi i zadachi komsomola," (Communist upbringing of youth and the tasks of the Komsomol), Partizat CK VKP(b) (1936), 9–10.

12 Jacob Emery, "The Land of Milk and Money: Communal Kitchens and Collactaneous Kinship in the Soviet 1920s," in *(M)Otherhood as Allegory*, eds Lisa Bernstein and Pamela Goco (Cambridge: Cambridge Scholar's Press, 2009), 162–172.

13 Evgeny Dobrenko, *The Political Economy of Socialist Realism* (New Haven and London: Yale University Press, 2007).

14 Ivan Gronsky, *Literaturnaya Gazeta*, 23 May 1932, cited in Helen Rappaport, *Joseph Stalin: A Biographical Companion* (Santa Barbara. ADC-Clio, 1999), 248.

15 N. Mashkova, "Proportsii, forma, tsvet" (Proportions, form, colour), *Obshchestvennitsa*, no. 9–10 (1936): 36.

16 D. Arkin, "Kultura Zhilishcha" (The culture of dwelling), *Obshchestvennitsa*, no. 2 (1936): 10.
17 Ibid.
18 Mashkova, "Proportsii, forma, tsvet," 36.
19 K. Kravchenko, "Interer, – ego arkhitektura i svetovoe oformlenie" (The interior – its architecture and lighting design), *Obshchestvennitsa*, 13 (1937): 19.
20 Mashkova, N. "Proportsii, forma, tsvet," 36.
21 Arkin, "Kultura zhilishcha," 11.
22 Anonymous, picture caption in *Obshchestvennitsa*, no. 1, (1936): 11.
23 G. Sushkin, "Vygonka rastenii" (Getting plants to open up), *Obshchestvennitsa*, no. 21 (1937): 50.
24 G. Sushkin, "Oformlenie posadok" (The design of plantings), *Obshchestvennitsa*, no. 8 (1937): 44.
25 Ibid.
26 G. Sushkin, "Tsvety i zelen na pervomayskikh torzhestvakh" (Flowers and greenery in the celebrations of the first of May), *Obshchestvennitsa*, no. 6 (1937): 31.
27 Ibid.
28 T. Ksanina, "Plafon dlya detskoy i spalnoy" (Lampshade for the nursery and the bedroom), *Obshchestvennitsa*, no. 8 (1937): 45.
29 L. Lipshtein and A. Lifshits, "Remont kvartiry" (Apartment renovation), *Obshchestvennitsa*, no. 2 (1936): 25.
30 Boris Groys, *The Total Art of Stalinism: Avant-Garde, Aesthetic Dictatorship, and Beyond* (New York: Verso, 2011).
31 Stovaratskii, A. *"Zerkalo"* (The Mirror) from *"Mama, pochitay!"* (Mother, Read to Me), *Obshchestvennitsa*, no. 11 (1938): 55.

6.1 Brigadier Rebrov, Lenin Medallist, in *How We Built the Metro*, 1935.

6

Golden calf, golden tooth

The hero

A man in a worker's coat smiles broadly, his golden tooth glinting. A heavy drill rests on his shoulder. The open collar of his coat reveals a dress shirt with a buttoned-down collar and a light-coloured tie. The man is "Brigadier Rebrov, recipient of the Order of Lenin," says the caption (Figure 6.1). The "brigadier" had been awarded the highest decoration in the Soviet Union, given to him presumably for his great contribution to the State and society. He was the epitome of the ideal Soviet citizen – an *udarnik*, an exceptionally enthusiastic labourer who breaks all production records. Rebrov relayed his zeal for advancing the socialist society in his construction work on the new underground transportation system in Moscow. He had been chosen for the award from the thousands who participated in freezing, drilling, cladding, and powering the entrails of the Soviet capital – the Moscow Metro, which opened in 1935 and was considered the most important project of the Second Five-Year Plan (1933–1937).

The worker's care for his appearance and the peculiar combination of work clothes, dress clothes, and a shiny smile demonstrated the dignity of the *udarnik* – a man with refined taste which went hand in hand with his struggle for communism and his passion for work. The photograph illustrates the book, *How We Built the Metro* (*Kak my stroili Metro*), that accompanied the opening of the Moscow Metro on 14 May 1935. The Metro was one of two big public works responsible for the colossal transformation of the Russian urban and rural landscape. The other, known as the "brother" of the Metro, was the Volga–Moscow canal, which was built with convict labour. The Metro was intended to symbolize the ethos of the working collective and the power of architecture to transform both the metropolis as well as the personal lives of the workers – a "victory" for the Soviet Union, as Lazar Kaganovich, the head of the Moscow Communist Party, called it. An immensely expensive and luxurious structure, the Metro also symbolized the self-sacrifice of the entire Soviet Union to a common goal, as well as the power of the State to unite and modernize the country during the Second Five-Year Plan. More importantly, in addition to contributing labour, the entire country contributed materials and money. The Metro is the golden calf of the Soviet Union, a precious and iconic object created by personal contributions and celebrating the socialist ethos – the common belief in the communist world to come.

Some 75,000 workers were employed in constructing the Metro. They belonged to crowds that flocked to Moscow in the late 1920s and early 1930s, escaping the famine-struck countryside. More than 4 million peasants moved to Soviet cities in 1931, and between 1928 and 1932 city populations increased by 11 million.[1] The population of Moscow alone grew from 2.2 million to 3.7 million in the four years of the First Five-Year Plan, from 1929 to 1932.[2] *Metrostroy*, the official government project of Metro construction, was supposed to employ this migrant populace in the great public work. The job, however, would be incomplete without creating a myth of construction that would negotiate the meaning of architecture and construction for creating an urban proletarian identity – transforming the peasant into an urbanite.

The book

How We Built the Metro played a key role in creating the myth of the Metro. Disseminated by a publishing house called History of Factories and Plants (*Istoriya fabrik i zavodov*), in a print run of 100,000 copies, it was preceded, three months earlier, by a volume titled *Stories of Metro Builders* (*Rasskazy stroiteley Metro*).[3] Both volumes were part of Maxim Gorky's project of writing histories of "little men."[4] The first one, *Stories*, is a compilation of individual accounts by the workers who came to the construction site of the Metro. They describe how, in the process of collective work on an architectural and infrastructural masterpiece, they transformed from peasants into Party-minded citizens of the metropolis. The second volume, *How We Built the Metro*, is a collective history of the Metro's construction, with accounts by the workers together with engineers, architects, and politicians. It is a definitive volume about how Soviet collective enthusiasm and the magnificence of Metro as its product redefined the notion of socialist urbanity.

How We Built the Metro is a work of official propaganda – an ideological project – but it is also an aesthetic one. The writers convey not only what the Metro meant to them as a symbol of communist political transformation but also their understanding of the Soviet, and communist, kind of magnificence and beauty. The metro was a magical, glorious, and magnificent world built and populated by people whose fervour for labour was matched only by their fervour for beauty. In a sense, political victory was supposed to be aesthetic victory – the construction not of the fastest, the most efficient, the best-planned Metro in the world, but the "most beautiful,"[5] the beauty of which showcases the "victory of socialism as a principle."[6]

The history, presumably written as the Metro was being built, begins with official speeches by Joseph Stalin and Lazar Kaganovich,[7] followed by chapters on the participation of Bolsheviks and *Komsomol* (All-Union Lenin Youth Communist League) in the construction of the Metro. The main body of the work, however, is a traversal of metro stations, in which descriptions of their appearance are interlaced with stories about different aspects of building. Prosaic passages with statistics and descriptions of construction operations are interrupted, as if by wells of electric light, by poetic descriptions of ecstatic experiences, of enchantment with the Metro's might and beauty. The magnificence of the ornament and textures in the finished Metro, the faces of enlightened and fascinated travellers, and the magic electrification embodied in the historic work are illustrated with sea-blue photographs.[8]

The content describing aspects of construction is extremely eclectic. There are chapters on the architecture of the Metro, written by architect Nikolai Kolli; a chapter on freezing the ground, "Nine Billion Calories of Cold"; and one on the escalator, called "Living Staircase." The basic textual form of each chapter is called the *otcherk*, which straddles literature and journalism. It conveys facts about Metro construction and documents its various episodes, and demonstrates the importance of the great work as a symbol of Soviet enthusiasm – an enthusiasm reflected in the style of the contributions. Authorship is blurred, as if the contributions were the work of a gigantic building collective. The number of authors cannot easily be determined. The chapters are frequently signed by several people, but the text itself comprises anecdotes related by others and interviews with workers. The series of *otcherks* that constitutes the history of Metro construction is imagined as a mass-created masterpiece that illustrates a confluence of destinies into one, an esprit de corps of socialist reconstruction.

Socialism's golden calf

The Moscow Metro was imagined as having been built by the entire country – the magnificent and stupefying product of the labour of millions. It was ultimately dedicated, according to Kaganovich, to the dignity and comfort of an even larger entity: the "millions of workers always and everywhere."[9] Accordingly, the entire country and, indeed, the entire proletarian world was meant to celebrate it. The book reports that on 15 May 1935, an ecstatic mass demonstration of synchronized movement in the streets of Moscow celebrated the opening of the first line of the subway (Figure 6.2). Workers sang the newly composed "Songs of Metro Conquerors." A live radio broadcast of events in a passenger car was transmitted to the entire Soviet Union. At the House

6.2 Workers' parade on the day of Metro opening, 15 May 1935, in *How We Built the Metro*.

Golden calf, golden tooth 159

6.3 Celebration at the House of Soviets, 14 May 1935, in *How We Built the Metro*.

of Soviets, celebratory speeches were delivered in front of a huge letter "M" situated in between portraits of Stalin and Kaganovich, sporting identical moustaches, and above a bust of Lenin (Figure 6.3).

Described by its builder-writers in *How We Built the Metro* as a system of "magnificent underground castles,"[10] the Metro embodied socialist modernity in many ways, and also signalled both Moscow's centrality and the prestige of the planned world of socialist industry. For Muscovites, the breathtaking vehicle of monumental propaganda combined urban transportation with "a significant rise of cultural standards," providing an education of "aesthetic sensibilities."[11] Pilgrims to the centre of Soviet political power and technological modernity who travelled the splendid underground corridors permeating the city could not miss the illuminated ceilings (Figures 6.4, 6.5), which one scholar compared to the ceilings of the Orthodox temples that the Metro was supposed to surpass.[12]

Each of the marble-clad stations, with their ample dimensions, precious marbles, rich decoration, and overall magnificence, was an anteroom, which, according to *How We Built the Metro*, evoked the experience of "being in a theatre lobby or the entrance hall of a first class hotel."[13] The primary effect of these anterooms, intended to "affect the observer

6.4 Krasnoselskaya station, in *How We Built the Metro.*

6.5 Ceiling of Lenin Library station, in *How We Built the Metro.*

within five minutes,"[14] was conveyed by electricity. Elaborate lighting embedded in the Metro's skies, its hidden "electrical heart," the text explains, animated the marble with a glimmering luminosity, creating a magical underworld. The builder-commentators considered that electricity's capacity to shift horizons was best incarnated in the rhythmic and silent flow of the escalator. They refer to it by an affectionate fairytale rhyme, "*lestnitsa chudesnitsa*," or the magic stairway.[15] As *How We Built the Metro* relates, these self-propelled stairs were transplanted from their capitalist American "homeland" and nurtured in socialist Moscow to become the most grandiose escalators in the world. The smoothness of their movement, in contrast to the "pulsating" and "intermittent" motion of elevators, was described as the fluid force of an invisible river. A ride on an escalator was envisioned as a mass "conversion" into metropolitan modernity.

Designing movement

The volume that preceded *How We Built the Metro*, called *Stories of Metro Builders*, set up the comparison between motion in the Metro and that of a river. According to this volume, the ecstatic energy of the delirious masses will convert Moscow into a metropolis:

> On the day when this book falls into the reader's hands, underground trains will be moving under the streets and squares of the great city. Thirteen marble palaces, erected under the ground, animated by the endless motion of passengers, the circulation of human stream, the din of Moscow – that delirious Niagara, which turns, day and night, the turbine of socialism ... To speak of the subway of Soviet Moscow is to speak of Moscow itself. It is to speak about the new spirit of the city, the expanded and magnified creativity of its citizens.[16]

In the image of a "delirious Niagara, which turns, day and night, the turbine of socialism," the obsession with directing the movement of the ecstatic socialist masses through a system of mass transit merges with the fascination with electricity. It is this intensified and regulated quality of movement, says the text, that finally made Moscow a city. This channelled, sped up, electrified motion reflected the electrified enthusiasm of the working millions.

The colossal work is not only the home of the formless, gushing human river, but also its product:

The life-building effort and the energy which gushed into Moscow with millions of human faiths, the spirit of people constructing socialism lead by the great Communist Party – this is the force which scraped new paths under the ground.[17]

To regulate movement was to change the identity of Muscovites: to turn them from disorganized, peasant-like individuals into rational, efficient creatures of socialist urbanity. In a classic of cultural criticism, written in 1927 during the preceding era of the New Economic Policy, Walter Benjamin observes that Moscow was a "gigantic village," a "rurally formless" ecology, a countryside settlement "playing hide and seek with the city."[18] Moscow in winter was characterized by a "backward state of traffic" and a "close mingling of people and things."[19] The traffic was mostly sleighs, set low to the ground, with people on them coming up against each other and things as they pass in the silent bustle of the snow-covered capital. Cars are few, writes Benjamin, "used only for weddings and funerals and for accelerated government."[20] The author's passage through the city on a sleigh is a passage through the set of a quiet, snow-covered market. It is a passage between goods: picture books, paper kites and fans, wooden toys, wooden spoons, baskets; a parrot; stuffed birds, clothes hangers, cakes, scrap iron, accordions, icons. The journey through a rurally formless Moscow was a winding passage through a sprawling offering of objects.

The First Five-Year Plan, which began a year after Benjamin's report, not only spelled the end of small business ownership and petty trade. It was also the beginning of an effort to channel the mobility of people by introducing internal passports – the militarization of society. It was a period of industrialization, of new ideas about the efficiency and speed of movement. The most important change was the introduction of city planning, made within the context of the re-collectivization of the economy during the First Five-Year Plan. Kaganovich, the godfather of the Metro, Secretary of the Central Committee of the Communist Party, and the head of the Moscow Division of the Communist Party from 1930 to 1935, wrote in the "Internal Planning of Cities" that the Duma had intended to plan the city during the 1920s, but could not because of the interests of private property. By the late 1920s, all city property was in government hands, and city planning on a large scale could begin. While the fundamental difference between socialist and capitalist cities is between planning and the chaos of the market,[21] Kaganovich says

Golden calf, golden tooth 163

that the difference is not just between village and city, a planned versus chaotic environment, but between designs of sobriety and ones of drunkenness:

> Let us take for an old city, for example, Moscow. We all know that cities were built in a random manner, especially merchant cities. When you walk down Moscow side-streets and passages, you get the impression that all these little passages were plotted by a drunk builder.[22]

For Kaganovich, it is the merchant, petty-bourgeois city that is inebriated. The new city of sobriety is the city of socialist centralized planning, based on a "scientific-technical approach."[23] This planned Moscow was a child of the Second Five-Year Plan (1932–1937). Principal directions for the plan were fixed at the third regional conference of the All-Russian Communist Party (Bolsheviks) (VKP(b)) in January 1932. The City Direction of Architecture and Planning (APU) created a general scheme by the beginning of 1933. It was modified in accordance to ongoing works to be completed in 1935, to fix a concentric scheme, with four radial boulevards dividing Moscow into districts and a ring delineating the boundaries of the city centre.

Blinding beauty

But it was not the spectacular vistas that became the symbol of new Moscow, as had happened, for example, in Haussmann's Paris, in the context of nineteenth-century bourgeois speculation and urban spectacle. Before the Moscow city plan was implemented, the government had finished the Metro, a labour of clandestine burrowing underneath Moscow. While the Metro was all about rapid, efficient movement, it also offered, instead of vistas, spaces of limited depth and, in cases described in *How We Built the Metro*, the sensation of blindness. Magnificent metro technology is experienced in a trance, explains one worker, and the worker goes blind with excitement. That worker describes the urban space beneath the parallel world of broad boulevards and their spectacular vistas:

> Do you know what technological passions are? [...]
>
> They are life at its extreme!
>
> I have been in Moscow for three years, and I know almost nothing but its centre. I have never been to a store – I just sometimes see them in a flash from the window of a racing car.

My world is the Metro.
When I go around the tunnel, I *do not see it.*
For me, it is only *time,* enveloped in *spatial* forms.[24]

This "time enveloped in spatial forms" was not a materialization of industrial rationality but, in many ways, the materialization of a world built by a drunken builder. The moving trains and magic escalators were enveloped in a mosaic of sculpture, wall tiles, shimmering lights, and ornament inspired by agricultural flora, disorienting as well as dazzling the passenger. The Metro was a phantasmagoria, a world that demonstrates the power of infinite transformation and the plasticity of the material world subject to the power of imagination. This is precisely what Kaganovich, who became the Metro's namesake, considered the most important aspect of the Metro's socialist beauty: the Metro was not simply a practical victory of socialism, but a victory of "socialism as a principle," which was an aesthetic victory as Kaganovich explained in his speech at the Metro's opening.[25] The Metro was, according to contemporary accounts, better than any Metro in existence. In reality, though, it was technologically inferior to many Western systems; the bureaucrat's main idea was that the Metro was aesthetically superior.[26] In the capitalist society, Kaganovich argued, spaces of everyday transit are drab and monotonous, but in socialism there is no monotony or uniformity; each station is different, and thus a source of pride and joy. The indulgence in the glamour of communal wealth is an indulgence in the infinite variety of form, a variety that, according to Kaganovich, countered capitalist claims that life under socialism is life in military barracks.

On 1 May 1934, Kaganovich, according to a probably apocryphal tale in *How We Built the Metro,* called the architects on the phone. The book relates the conversation: "'Dear Comrades,' he said, 'we should make Metro stations.' 'What is the deadline?' 'Twenty-five days.' 'Which station?' 'You, Comrade Kolli, Kirovskaya, you, comrade, that one.' 'What kind of stations shall we make?' 'Beautiful stations.'"[27] Kaganovich randomly distributed the stations among architects whose aesthetic choices differed. Chechulin's Komsomolskaya station featured capitals in the shape of wheat and decorated with hammers and sickles (Figure 6.6), an architecture of a new socialist order; and Likhtenberg and Dushkin's Dvorets Sovetov station conveys monumentality through sober and minimal means, inspired, according to the authors, by the simple

Golden calf, golden tooth

6.6 Capitol at Komsomolskaya station, in *How We Built the Metro*.

monumentality of the Egyptian temple, the ceiling supported by the stylized version of the column with a papyrus capitol (Figure 6.7).

However, all stations had in common a "beautiful architectural cloak" that many accounts in the collective history remarked upon.[28] "We were told," testify the architects, "there are such and such forms and such and such ceilings – try to dress them."[29] This dress consisted of marble, the symbol of collective opulence. The architects write about the marble they used – about how difficult it was to excavate it, how difficult it was for the architect to select the right type from swatches, how it had to be measured and calculated, how inspired one had be to invent detail. The architects demonstrated their expertise with marble through choices of colour and illumination and by creating sensations of lightness, expanse, and solidity.

Extravagant marbles were brought to the site from across the entire Soviet Union. The provenance of the marbles was a central architectural and mythological concern. In one of the chapters of *How We Built the Metro*, a man by the name of I. D. Gortseridze writes that he was assigned to write a chapter on a Metro station, in the capacity of a person coming from Shosha, the Georgian village where the station's red marble comes from. The author relates this fact with great tenderness and pride in the contribution of his village. The obsessively fetishized cladding of the

6.7 Likhtenberg and Dushkin, Dvorets Sovetov station (renamed "Kropotkinskaya"), in *Stroitelstvo Moskvy*, 1935.

metropolitan summarized the geography of the entire Soviet Union and its sacrificed wealth.

In the 1920s Lenin famously proclaimed, "Communism is Soviet power plus the electrification of the whole country." Electricity lent the cloak of the Metro "magnificence and light"; it created an "aura of lyrical soulfulness."[30] The ultimate sources of aesthetic pleasure were not primarily the Metro's forms, but its surfaces. Illuminated by electricity, surfaces were endowed with the capacity to radiate the aura of socialist construction, to lift the spirit and to stupefy. The main "impression" of the Metro's architecture is beyond sculptural form – the effect of the lustre and ripple of the illuminated surface:

> Marble! Mastering the proportions and elements of the environment, the passenger now experiences a new impression – colour and tint. He has just observed the station as a sculpture, from the aspect of its volumes. Now he sees the station as a work of illumination. Soft gleaming tones of marble ripple as the spectator pilots his gaze from column to column.[31]

"Illumination" of marbles created a cloak that shone like gold. This sparkle was the most elemental image of the immeasurable wealth of the working millions that the Metro was supposed to embody. In his speech at the opening of the Metro, Kaganovich hails the appearance of the marble column and its "flame" as the glory of workers' and peasants' fortune:

> The peasant, the worker, can see in the metropolitan, in those flames, in those marble columns, not only marble, not only a marvellous technical structure. He sees in the Metro a realization of his might, of his power. In the past only landowners, only the rich utilized marble. And now the power is ours, this construction is for us – workers and peasants – these are our marble columns, our own, Soviet, socialist. (Applause, cries Hurray!)[32]

The haptic sensorium

It was not only marble columns and walls that were supposed to gleam. The design of the train car also demonstrated a delicate attention to surfaces aimed at making them shimmery and effervescent. The idea of architecture as surface management and the production of gleam is elaborated in an article, "Architecture of the Metro car," written in 1933 by the designer S. M. Kravets and published in the journal dedicated to the building of the Metro. Kravets explains the essence of architecture as the light "spectrum," composed of "mirror glass, metal elements plated with nickel, polished wood and the matte surface of the ceiling, the natural wood of the seats, the red wood of walls, the silver reflections of the nickel surface."[33] Design, at all scales, was the design of the sparkly cloak. A photograph in *How We Built the Metro*, featuring two Metro officers visiting the new car on the day of the Metro opening, shows the inspection of gleam – not only by eye, but also by touch (Figure 6.8). An officer with a wrench in his hand, as if he has just completed fixing the car, uses his other hand to touch the nickel-plated surface of a railing to fully test its cleanliness, smoothness, and lustre. The iridescent beauty of the Metro, which materialized the life-giving power of electricity, collective opulence, and immense investment of collective labour, could be literally grasped on the scale of the tiniest detail.

This understanding of architecture as an assemblage of surfaces perceived by both touch and sight – a design that is not about visual form but about warmth, shine, and texture – emerges as part of an avant-garde practice that predates the Metro. The difference between capitalist and socialist modernism lay in the way architecture was perceived. The capitalist modern was merely a revolution of visual form; socialist modernism was expected to go beyond the optical. Soviet design of the

6.8 Inspection of metro cars, in *How We Built the Metro*.

future would enter the realm of the supra-visual; articulating new forms of social life, it would articulate a new sensuality, engaging the *haptic*, visual-tactile sensorium. This, at least, was the vision of one of the pioneers of Soviet constructivism, Moisei Ginzburg, as elaborated in his treatise of 1934, *Housing*. Ginzburg criticized Western modernism because rather than doing away with ornament, it had merely replaced it with other visual effects. The constructivist architect took Le Corbusier as an example of this tendency, proclaiming him a relatively conservative formalist:

> Despite the plastic clarity and richness of spatial thought, as well as the correct understanding of contemporary industry as the only way of building housing, Le Corbusier nevertheless did not explore the potentials of housing construction beyond successful visual forms. In place of illusionist decoration and ornament of his architectural predecessors, Le Corbusier offers a brilliant formal language expressing new spatial concepts. But his work is no more radical than this.[34]

There was, in Ginzburg's opinion, a radical modernist problem which "no one [apart from the author] had yet tried to solve in the country."[35] His focus was no longer on colour-light-spatial (*tsvetosvetoprostranstvennye*) problems. The radically modern architectural turn was the exploration of texture, the problem of "visually tactile perception," the problem of touch, which "by extension corresponded to conditional reflexes and also visual perception."[36] For Ginzburg, what were essential for the architecture of socialist domesticity was the production, selection, and design of textures, the "sensations of coldness, of warmth, of smoothness, of roughness, and similar material qualities," and the exploration of "the solidity of colour."[37] Exploring tactile-visual perception was essential to housing design, and involved a sophisticated sensibility.

Ginzburg thought that visually tactile perception was important for private habitation, for "staying in a dwelling for long periods of time."[38] But one year after the publication of *Housing*, the Moscow Metro was opened. Unlike the home, it was a public space. It was not a home of the socialist family, but the home of the electrical train. In the eyes of its builders, however, the aesthetic of this project is a strangely Ginzburgian one of haptic perception.

Developing the Metro style

There is a strong connection between the aesthetic of the Metro and the aesthetic of everyday life. The haptic qualities of Metro marbles were translated into qualities of workers' intimate environments and personal appearance, as part of the "acculturation" process to which the workers were subjected. The ongoing process of turning "illiterate, backward, uncivilized people, even hooligans, into vanguard, informed toilers of the great socialist building site"[39] is a major element of the period of Stalinist planned economy. Metro construction was its poster case. The power of the Party to recreate nature in Moscow's underground was paralleled by its power to turn vagabond individuals from the countryside into cultured urbanites, and transform them into a conscious collective subject of historical construction. Acculturation, the process of creating what the Russians called *kulturnost*, entailed developing a taste for art and indulging in the works of romantic poets and music, but most importantly, it involved a change of everyday habits.[40] This process of change seemed to encompass a very wide range of practices. Among them were teaching basic literacy, personal hygiene, and developing an expertise in domesticity as well as an interest in newspapers describing world affairs (Figure 6.9). Tens of thousands of workers, housed in temporary wooden barracks on the outskirts of Moscow, were trained

6.9 Dzerzhinsky Square station, entry hall, in *How We Built the Metro*.

not to go to bed in dirty boots, to change sheets regularly, to use a book, a mirror, a lamp, a curtain. Workers were taught how to enjoy a game of chess in a city's "parks of culture and recreation" (Figure 6.10). The new urbanites were taught not to be afraid of trams and cars. They were taught to shower regularly and use the radio.

Acculturation was also a matter of developing a particular aesthetic approach to interior decoration and grooming. In *How We Built the Metro*, frequent topics of discussion are the whiteness of sheets and curtains, personal cleanliness, and the polish of floors and tables. This is not something present in the Metro treatise alone. An attention to the cleanliness, shine, colour, porosity, and touch of most intimate surfaces was ultimately the most important manifestation of culture mindedness in the early 1930s.[41] Cultural knowledge was at the time conceived as a combination of fashion, cleanliness, and domesticity, all described in terms of surface management. The presence of cultural consciousness was rendered visible in smoothly shaven faces, curtains, lampshades, and the emblematic white tablecloth. Until the late 1930s, when learning a classical body of knowledge came to define a cultured, edified citizen, "culture mindedness" or *kulturnost* had consisted of an evolving sense of decorum, which included a refined responsiveness to colours and textures.

Golden calf, golden tooth　　　　　　　　　　　　　　　　　　　　171

6.10　Shock workers resting, in *How We Built the Metro.*

The man with the golden tooth, Lenin Medalist Brigadier Rebrov, illustrates passages on acculturation in *How We Built the Metro* (Figures 6.1, 6.11). He is not only a record-breaking worker. He is also an example of acculturation. The gleam of the tooth reflects the gleam of Metro's surfaces. The appearance of the acculturated worker, his home, and the architecture of the Metro are all crisp shiny surfaces; the labour of constructing architecture and constructing oneself are one.

Labour's end

The Metro's shining surfaces materialized not just communal wealth, new notions of beauty and culture, but also collective labour. The workers were not simply depicted in the mosaics adorning the Metro (Figure 6.12). The aura of the Metro, reflected in the tactile-visual qualities of the workers' intimate environment and appearance, was a manifestation of labour itself and of the emotional, even erotic, relationship of the workers to their work. In particular, the gleam of the communist masterpiece is created by polishing and caressing marble surfaces. From *How we Built the Metro* we learn about the very moment in which workers encounter the end of labour, the moment in which the labour

6.11 The labour of our party is our literature: our combat and our Revolutionary work, in *How We Built the Metro*.

6.12 Mosaic at Komsomolskaya station, in *How we Built the Metro*.

of construction transforms into gentle, loving adulation of the magical surface:

> The night before the test drive of the trains, metro workers, exhausted by weeks' lack of sleep and incredibly excited, wandered around the gleaming underground palaces. Transportation authorities had already taken over. Metro officials in navy blue uniforms took control of the stations. Yet the builders, for whom the only thing left to do was to go to bed, could not take their eyes off their child [...] Secretly, they would rub a spotless marble plate with their sleeves, as if cleaning eyeglasses.[42]

The work of acculturation, of transforming the workers into New Women and New Men, was complete with the completion of the Metro, in which they left the traces and representations of self-transforming labour. The event signalling the completion of Metro construction – the arrival of a train – is cinematic:

> [The workers] pined, they loomed about from corner to corner, caressing their well-made environment with their eyes, recollecting the history of each meter, every yard of the tunnel and the station. At that moment, a faraway hum resounded. It grew louder in the tunnel's orifice, and finally embodied itself in a train, approaching the platform. The train was mirrored in the marble. Laughing and screaming with joy, girls and boys in overalls threw themselves at it. They realized that, crowning their work, is – a train, a train under Moscow. When it disappeared in the tunnel, they long stared behind it. The Metro exists. It is time for builders to leave.[43]

The workers were taught not only how to think as proletarians but also how to see the world, how to "caress the environment with their eyes," in the manner of enlightened urbanites. The Metro was the palatial home of the Soviet collective and the symbol of social progress. It was also a shimmering reflection of Soviet modernity. Like the shimmering and shifting image on the shiny marble wall of the Metro, architecture, on the monumental and the intimate scale alike, stood as a shimmering and shifting image of Soviet modernity, a mirror that reflected and refracted the appearance of Soviet progress and its protagonists.

Notes

1 Sheila Fitzpatrick, "The Great Departure: Rural-Urban Migration in the Soviet Union, 1929–33," in William G. Rosenberg and Lewis H. Siegebaum,

eds, *Social Dimensions of Soviet Industrialization* (Bloomington: Indiana University Press, 1993), 22.

2 Mike O' Mahoni, "Archaeological fantasies: Constructing history on the Moscow Metro," *The Modern Language Review*, 98, no. 1 (Jan., 2003): 142.

3 Vladimir Paperny, *Culture Two: Architecture in the Age of Stalin*, transl. John Hill and Roann Barris in collaboration with the author (Cambridge: Cambridge University Press, 2002), 18. The author establishes that the book was published exactly five weeks after the opening of the first subway, and was thus probably being written at the same time as construction was proceeding, a notion plausible in light of the fervent activity of literary *kruzhoks* at the construction site.

4 See Katerina Clark, "Little Heroes and Big Deeds: Literature Responds to the First Five-Year Plan," in *Cultural Revolution in Russia*, Sheila Fitzpatrick, ed. (Bloomington and London: Indiana University Press, 1978).

5 "Most beautiful" is routinely used to describe both the Metro and each individual station in this book. The fact that the Metro is the best in the world is witnessed by the American George Morgan, one of the Metro's principal engineers. See George Morgan, "Luchshi' v mire" ("Best in the World"), in *Rasskazy stroiteley metro (Accounts of Metro Builders)* (Moscow: Istoriya fabrik i zavodov, 1935).

6 "*Pobeda metro—pobeda sotsializma: Rech tovarisha L. M. Kaganovicha na torzhestvenom zasedanii, posvyashchennom pusku metropolitena, 14 maya 1935 goda*" (The victory of the Metro is a victory of socialism: The speech of comrade L. M. Kaganovich on the ceremony dedicated to the opening of the metro, 14 May 1935), *Kak my stroili metro*, XXVII.

7 Lazar Kaganovich supervised Metro construction as the most prominent Party functionary of the 1930s and close associate of Stalin. From 1935 to 1955 the underground system was named after him, as the *Metropoliten imeni L.M. Kaganovicha* (Metro by the name of L.M. Kaganovich).

8 "The struggle with nature under Moscow" is a formulaic way of referring to these works in *How We Built the Metro*.

9 "*Pobeda metro—pobeda sotsializma,*" XXVII.

10 K. F. Starostin and others, "Bolsheviki na Metrostroie" (Bolsheviks of the Metrostroi), *Kak my stroili metro*, 38.

11 Ibid., 41.

12 This was first mentioned in scholarship by Andrew Jenks in the article, "A Metro on the Mount: The underground as a church of Soviet civilization," *Technology and Culture*, 41, no. 4 (Oct., 2000): 697–724.

13 Efim Reznichenko, *Dni i gody metrostroia (Days and Years of Metrostroi)*, cited by Jenks, "A Metro on the Mount," 713.

14 *Kak my stroili metro*, 196.

15 L. A. Ostrovsky, "Zhivaya lestnitsa" (The living stairway), in *Kak my stroili metro*.
16 Aleksandr Kosarev and others, "*Ob avtorah etoy knigi*," in *Rasskazy stroitelei metro*, 8.
17 Ibid.
18 Ibid., 112, 125, 124.
19 Ibid., 100, 112.
20 Ibid., 100.
21 L. M. Kaganovich, *Za sotsialisticheskuyu rekonstruktsiyu Moskvy i gorodov SSSR—pererabotannaia stenograma doklada na iyunskom plenume TSKVKP (b)* (For the socialist reconstruction of Moscow and cities in the USSR—edited stenogram of the speech on the June session of the Central Committee of the All-Soviet Communist Party (b)) (Moscow: Moskovsky rabochy, 1931), 65.
22 Ibid.
23 Ibid.
24 A. I. Gertner, "O smelosti" (On Courage), *Rasskazy stroitelei metro* (*Stories of Metro Builders*) (Moscow: Istoriya fabrik i zavodov, 1935), 116–117. Emphasis in the original.
25 "Pobeda metro," *Kak my stroili metro*, XXVII.
26 In 1935 it transported 177,000 passengers daily, in comparison to the New York subway, which transported 1.8 million. The maximum speed of its trains was only 32 miles per hour, compared to 45 miles per hour in the much older New York subway, and the average speed was 17 to 18 miles per hour, compared to 25 in New York. See Jenks, "A Metro on the Mount," 304–305.
27 N. Y. Kolli, "Arkhitektura Metro," (Architecture of the Metro), *Kak my stroili metro*, 178.
28 I. D. Gortseridze, "Stantsiya Krasnye Vorota" (Station Krasnye Vorota), *Kak my stroili metro*, 30.
29 N. Y. Kolli, "Arkhitektura Metro," 177.
30 Ibid.
31 Kosarev and others, "Ob avtorah etoi knigi," 9–10.
32 "*Pobeda metro—pobeda sotsializma*," XXVII.
33 S. M. Kravets, "Arkhitektura vagona metro," *Metrostroi*, no. 7 (1933): 20.
34 Moisei Ginzburg, *Zhilishche* (*Housing*) (Moscow: Gosudarstvennoe nauchno-technicheskoe izdatelstvo stroitelnoi industrii i sudostroeniya, 1934), 22.
35 Ibid., 96.
36 Ibid.
37 Ibid.
38 Ibid.

39 K. F. Starostin and others, "Zabota o zhivom cheloveke" (Concern for the living man), in "Bolsheviki na Metrostroie" (Bolsheviks in Metrostroi), in *Kak my stroili metro*, 38.
40 According to Vadim Volkov, *kulturnost* is a notion developed from the German opposition between *Kultur* and *Zivilisation* and was employed to signify the mass enlightenment as intelligentsia's propagation and transmission of national material culture. It was a product of the Slavophile discourse of the 1880s. In the 1930s, the agent of *kulturnost* was the Communist Party, more appropriate for the partisan project then, for instance an academic institution (Volkov, "The Concept of *Kul'turnost'*: Notes on the Stalinist Civilizing Process," in *Stalinism—New Directions* (London and New York: Routlege, 2000), 211–212).
41 Volkov, "The Concept of *Kul'turnost*," 217–222.
42 M. O. Rohvarger, "Stantsiya Smolenskaya Ploshad'" (Station Smolensky Square), *Kak my stroili metro*, 457.
43 Ibid., 458.

Conclusion

The story of Soviet architecture is, in many ways, a story of builders who created socialism's wondrous image – their real and imagined identities, such as that of the politically and aesthetically enlightened builder – and then left the scene. These people "built" socialism in the most literal way – by erecting, digging, and assembling structures. "Building" socialism was also a metaphor for pursuing the goals of the communist revolution, becoming a New Man (or woman) along the way. As the idea of international proletarian revolution, which drove the revolutionary events of October 1917, was gradually replaced by the idea of socialism in one country, promoted by Stalin, the productivist ethos of the built environment was replaced, by the 1930s, by an ethos of admiration for the Soviet State as the most progressive country in the world. Throughout the 1920s and the 1930s, however, ideological awareness was purposefully coupled with new interpretations of the material environment. Creating new people – proletarian actors; ardent workers; socially minded housewives; sober, clean, and responsible citizens; communist urbanites – entailed creating a concoction of real environments in which they lived as well as myths about these environments. These myths posited the existence of ideal Soviet citizens of the future, who were in the process of becoming. Looking at changes in the way the identity of citizens and the kind of spaces they inhabit are conceived helps explain how the understanding of communism shifted. Architecture of the Soviet Union involved constant cycles of myth translated into design, of design into physical reality, and of reality back into myth. The complex chain of these translations defined and produced ideological transformation.

The notion of "New People" in the communist realm was, in a sense, a mirage. Soviet citizens never became as free and as enlightened as the myth about the New Man promised. Furthermore, this myth often functioned as an instrument of governance and a tool of oppression. But the fabrication of this myth and its spatial manifestations was not a monolithic totalitarian enterprise completely controlled by those in power. As we have seen, the development of this myth entailed, apart from big ideological and political shifts, such as the transition from "Leninism" to "Stalinism," a process of incremental change. This process depended on Party decrees of changes in government policy but also, and more importantly, on a constant reinterpretation of the communist master narrative. Architecture, as the art of both conceptualizing and constructing the physical environment, reflected the totalitarian systems of values and beliefs. But its creators – architects, architectural enthusiasts, housewives, workers, statisticians, and politicians – often produced peculiar and quirky interpretations of communism's officially presented image. Their environmental production was often not the result of obedience or allegiance to the State but of enthusiasm, hopefulness, projection, aspirations. As the case studies examined in this book demonstrate, in the process of navigating between texts, images, and objects, each individual "construction" of socialism was slightly off, slightly weird, slightly eccentric. Even if Soviet architects, para-architects, and architectural enthusiasts thoroughly participated in a collective endeavour, defined by and articulated in the language of power and the dominant system of values and beliefs, this ideological space of Soviet architecture was in no way homogenous.

This point is most clearly evident in the heterogeneity of ideological practices, manifested in the slippages and idiosyncrasies described in this book that frequently render the often grave story of Soviet life also amusing. The architect who designs portable wings for going to work; the earnest housewife who tries to get fat to support the idea that that the Soviet Union is a world of plenty; the statistician who tries to make everyone more productive by streamlining singing, hunting, napping, and playing chequers; the poet who decides that factory management is the ultimate poem; the designer who thinks that he will destroy the capitalist institution of marriage by allocating a single Murphy bed to each worker . . . The zeal of these people, inspired by their belief in utopia as an alternative to the drab and dreary socialist reality of the present, renders their projects fantastic, puzzling, and even sublime. The

Soviet State perverted the modernist dream of freedom and progress; Soviet architectural enthusiasts would pervert this perversion, and the level of this new perversion is the true measure of freedom. They could not have crossed the boundaries of their historical milieu. But they were able to invest it and reinvest it with hopefulness, which is, in the end, modernism's most potent legacy.

Select bibliography

Alpers, Boris. *Teatr sotsialnoi maski (Theater of the Social Mask)*. Moscow: 1931.
Andreev, Andrey. *Kommunisticheskoe vospitanie molodezhi i zadachi komsomola, (Communist Upbringing of Youth and the Tasks of the Komsomol)*. Moscow: Partizat CK VKP(b), 1936: 9–10.
Anon. "Individualnoe zhilishche no. 30" (Individual house no. 30), *Sovremennaya arkhitektura* 6 (Nov. 1930): 13.
Anon. "Sharlatanstvo ili glupost'" (Charlatanism or stupidity). *Rabochaya Moskva* 196 (3 Nov., 1922).
Arkin, D. "Kul'tura Zhilishcha" (The culture of dwelling). *Obshchestvennitsa* 2 (1936): 10–11.
Arvatov, Boris. *"Byt i kultura veschi"*. (Everyday life and the culture of the thing (Toward the formulation of the question)), transl. Kristina Kiaer. *October* 81 (Summer 1996): 119–128.
Arvatov, Boris. *Ob agit ai proz isskustve (On Agitation and Production Art)* Moscow: Federatsiya, 1930.
Bakhtin, Mikhail. "Forms of Time and the Chronotope in the Novel." In *The Dialogic Imagination*, trans. Caryl Emerson and Michael Holquist. Houston: University of Texas Press, 1981: 84–258.
Balmas-Neary, Rebecca. "Flowers and Metal: The Soviet 'Wife-Activists' Movement' and Stalin-era Culture and Society 1934–1941." PhD dissertation, Columbia University, 2002.
Belakhov, I. "Uhod za kozhey litsa" (Care of facial skin). *Obshchestvennitsa* 11 (1937): 31.
Belakhov, I. "Uhod za volosami," (Hair care). *Obshchestvennitsa* 16 (1937): 31–32.
Benvenutti, Francesco. "Industry and purge in the Donbass 1936–1937," *Europe-Asia Studies* 45, no. 1 (1993): 68–69.
Bergman, Jay. "Valerii Chkalov: The Soviet pilot as a new Soviet man." *Journal of Contemporary History* 33, no. 1 (Jan. 1998): 140.

Bogdanov, Alexander. *Red Star*, trans. Charles Rougle. Bloomington: Indiana University Press, 1984.

Bogdanov, Alexander. "O tendentsiyah proletarskoi kulturi (Otvet A. Gastevu" (On the tendencies in proletarian culture (A response to A. Gastev)). *Proletarskaia Kultura* nos 9–10 (1919): 46–52.

Bogdanov, Igor Alekseevich. *Tri veka peterburgskoi bani. (Three Centuries of the Petersburg Bath)*. Saint Petersburg: Isskustvo-SPB, 2000.

Bohn, Willard. "Poetics of flight: Futurist aeropoesia." *MLN*, 121, no. 1 (2006): 207–224.

Boym, Svetlana. *Common Places: Mythologies of Everyday Life in Russia*. Cambridge, Mass.: Harvard University Press, 1994.

Boym, Svetlana and Adam Bartos. *Kosmos: A Portrait of the Russian Space Age*. New York: Princeton Architectural Press, 2001.

Buchloh, Benjamin H. D. "From faktura to factography." *October* 30 (Fall 1984): 82–119.

Clark, Katerina. "Little Heroes and Big Deeds: Literature Responds to the First Five-Year Plan." In *Cultural Revolution in Russia*, Sheila Fitzpatrick ed. Bloomington and London: Indiana University Press, 1978.

Clark, Katerina. *Petersburg, Crucible of the Cultural Revolution*. Cambridge, Mass.: Harvard University Press, 1995.

Clark, Katerina. *Moscow the Fourth Rome: Stalinism, Cosmopolitanism and the Evolution of Soviet Culture, 1931–1941*. Cambridge, Mass.: Harvard University Press, 2011.

Cohen, Jean-Louis. *The Future of Architecture since 1889: A Worldwide History*. New York: Phaidon, 2012.

Davies, R. W., Tauger, M. B., and Wheatcroft, S. G. "Stalin, grain stocks, and the famine of 1932–1933." *Slavic Review* 54, no. 3 (Autumn 1995): 642–657.

Deleuze, Giles and Felix Guattari. *Capitalisme et Schizophrénie: Mille Plateaux*. Paris: Éditions de Minuit, 1980.

Dobrenko, Evgeny. *Political Economy of Socialist Realism*. New Haven: Yale University Press, 2007.

Emery, Jacob. "The Land of Milk and Money: Communal Kitchens and Collactaneous Kinship in the Soviet 1920s." In *(M)Otherhood as Allegory*, Lisa Bernstein and Pamela Goco eds. Cambridge, UK: Cambridge Scholar's Press, 2009: 162–172.

Fitzpatrick, Sheila. *The Cultural Front: Power and Culture in Revolutionary Russia*. Ithaca: Cornell University Press, 1992.

Fitzpatrick, Sheila. *Everyday Stalinism: Ordinary Life in Extraordinary Times*. New York: Oxford University Press, 1999.

Fitzpatrick, Sheila. "The Great Departure: Rural-Urban Migration in the Soviet Union, 1929–33." In *Social Dimensions of Soviet Industrialization*. William G.

Rosenberg and Lewis H. Siegebaum eds. Bloomington: Indiana University Press, 1993.

Fitzpatrick, Sheila and Yuri Slezkine, eds, *In the Shadow of the Revolution: Life Stories of Russian Women from 1917 to the Second World War*. Princeton: Princeton University Press, 2000.

Gastev, Aleksey. *Poeziya rabochego udara (Poetry of the Factory Floor)*. Petrograd: Proletkul't, 1918.

Gastev, Aleksey. *Kak nado rabotat: Prakticheskoe vvedenie v nauku organizatsii truda. (How to Work: Practical Introduction into the Scientific Organization of Labor)*. Moscow: Ekonomika, 1966.

Gerovitch, Slava. "'New Soviet Man' inside machine: Human engineering, spacecraft design, and the construction of communism." *Osiris* 22, no. 1 (2007): 135–157.

Gertner, A. I. "O smelosti" (On courage). *Rasskazy stroitelei metro (Stories of Metro Builders)*. Moscow: Istoriya fabrik i zavodov, 1935: 116–117.

Gilarovskaya, Nadezhda Vladimirovna. *Teatralno-dekoratsionnoe iskusstvo za 5 let (Theatre-decorative Art in 5 Years)*. Kazan: Kombinat izdatelstva i pechati, 1924.

Ginzburg, Moisei. *Zhilishche (Housing)*. Moscow: Gosudarstvennoe nauchno-technicheskoe izdatelstvo stroitel'noi industrii i sudostroenma, 1934.

Goldenberg, N. A. *Banya dlya voisk i dlya narodnykh mass v gigienicheskom, sanitarnom, lechebnom i ekonomicheskom otnoshenii: kratkie ukazaniya dlya vrachei; dlya voyskovikh chastey, gorodskikh i zemskikh upravlenii; dlya shkol, fabrik, zavodov, i dr. (The Bath for Armies and for Popular Masses – its Sanitary, Medical and Economical Aspects: Short Instructions for Doctors, for Military Units, for Municipal and District Governments: For Schools, Factories, Plants, etc.)* Saint Petersburg: Tip. E. Evdokimova, 1898.

Gortseridze, I. D. "Stantsiya Krasnye Vorota" (Station Krasnye Vorota). In *Kak my stroili Metro (How We Built the Metro)*. Moscow: Istoriya fabrik i zavodov, 1935.

Groys, Boris. *Total Art of Stalinism: Aesthetic Dictatorship and Beyond*. Princeton: Princeton University Press, 1992.

Groys, Boris. "Proizvedenie iskusstva kak nefunkcionalnaya mashina" (The work of art as a non-functional machine). In *Vladimir Tatlin–Leben, Werk, Wirkung* Jürgen Harten, ed. Koln: Du Mont, 1993.

Harms, Danil. *Izabrannoe (Selections)*. ed. George Gibian. Wurzburg: Jal-verlag, 1974.

Hays, Michael. *Hejduk's Chronotope*. Princeton: Princeton Architectural Press, 1996.

Hudson, Hugh D. *Blueprints and Blood: The Stalinization of Soviet Architecture*. Princeton: Princeton University Press, 1993.

Ignatov, Sergey. "*AKI, GITIS I KAT*." 1922. RGALI, Fond 963, Opis 1.

Ikonnikov, Andrei. *Russian Architecture of the Soviet Period*, trans. Lev Lyapin. London: Collets, 1988.
Ivanov, V. P. "Istoriya chastnicheskogo Bannogo tresta" (The history of the private bath trust). *Voprosy kommunalnogo khoziaistva* 7 (July 1930): 62.
Jenks, Andrew "A Metro on the Mount: The underground as a church of Soviet civilization." *Technology and Culture* 41, no. 4 (Oct. 2000): 697–724.
Johansson, Kurt. *Aleksej Gastev: Proletarian Bard of the Machine Age*. Stockholm: Almqvist & Wiksell International, 1983.
Kaganovich, Lazar M. Za sotsialisticheskuyu rekonstruktsiyu Moskvy i gorodov SSSR – pererabotannaya stenograma doklada na iyunskom plenume TSKVKP (b) (For the socialist reconstruction of Moscow and cities in the USSR – edited shorthand recording of the speech on the June session of the Central Committee of the All-Soviet Communist Party (b)). Moscow: Moskovskii rabochii, 1931.
Kaganovich, Lazar M. "Pobeda metro–pobeda sotsializma" (The victory of the Metro is a victory of socialism). In *Kak my stroili metro (How We Built the Metro)*: XXVII.
Kamensky, Vasily. *Ego-moya biografiya velikogo futurista*. Moscow: Kitovras, 1918.
Kiaer, Kristina. "Boris Arvatov's Socialist objects", *October* 81 (Summer 1997): 105–118.
Kiaer, Kristina. *Imagine no Possessions*. Cambridge, Mass.: MIT Press, 2005.
Kolli, Nikolai. "Arkhitektura Metro" (Architecture of the Metro). In *Kak my stroili Metro (How We Built the Metro)*. Moscow: Istoriya fabrik i zavodov, 1935.
Kopp, Anatole. *Town and Revolution: Soviet Architecture and City Planning 1917–1935*, trans. Thomas E. Burton. London: Thames and Hudson, 1970.
Kosarev, Aleksandr. "Ob avtorakh etoi knigi" (From the authors of this book). In *Kak my stroili Metro (How We Built the Metro)*. Moscow: Istoriya fabrik i zavodov, 1935.
Kosarev, Aleksandr, ed. *Rasskazy stroitelei metro (Stories of Metro Builders)*. Moscow: Istoriya fabrik i zavodov, 1935.
Kovalev, L. and Aleksei Shchusev, ed. *Metro. Sbornik posvyashchenii pusku moskovskogo metropolitena (Metro: Anthology Dedicated to the Opening of the Moscow Metropolitan)*. Moscow: Publishing house of the journal *Rabochaya Moskva*, 1935.
Kozlov, Dimitrii. "Aleksandr Nikolskii i suprematisty" (Alexandr Nikolsky and the Suprematists). *Sbornik trudov fakulteta istorii iskusstv Evropeiskogo universiteta v Sankt-Peterburge*. (Works produced by the faculty of art history at the European University in St Petersburg). 2007: 98–114.
Kravchenko, K. "Interer, ego arkhitektura i svetovoe oformlenie" (The Interior – its architecture and lighting design). *Obshchestvennitsa* 13 (1937): 18–19.
Kravchenko, K. "Ob uyute" (On comfort). *Obshchestvennitsa* 17–18: 30–31.
Kravets, S. M. "Arkhitektura vagona metro" (The architecture of the Metro car). *Metrostroi* 7 (1933): 20.

Krementsov, Nikolay. *A Martian Stranded on Earth: Alexander Bogdanov, Blood Transfusions, and Proletarian Science*. Chicago: Chicago University Press, 2011.

Ksanina, T. "Plafon dlia detskoi i spal'noi" (Lampshade for the nursery and the bedroom). *Obshchestvennitsa* 8 (1937): 45–46.

Kudryakov, Ivan. "Dvorets zdorovya" (Palace of health). *Kultura i byt* 13 (1930): 67.

Ladinskii, Anatoly S. "Ratsionalizatsiya proektirovaniya tait v sebe ogromnye vozmozhnosti ekonomii: Kogda tselesoobrazna postroika zdanii bez pryamogo osveshcheniya?" (The rationalization of design hides great potential for economizing: When is the construction of buildings without direct lighting purposeful?) *Stroitelstvo Moskvy* 1 (Jan. 1932): 30.

Law, Alma H. "Meyerhold's 'The Magnanimous Cuckold.'" *The Drama Review: TDR* 26, 1, Historical Performance Issue (Spring, 1982): 61–86.

Lipshtein, L. and Lifshits A. "Remont kvartiry" (Apartment renovation). *Obshchestvennitsa* 2 (1936): 25.

Lissitsky, El. *Architecture for the World Revolution*, trans. Eric Dluhosch. Cambridge, Mass.: MIT Press, 1984.

Malevich, Kazimir. *The Non-Objective World: The Manifesto of Suprematism*. Mineola: Dover Publications, 2003.

Mashkova, N. "Proportsii, forma, tsvet" (Proportions, form, color). *Obshchestvennitsa* 9–10 (1936): 36–37.

Meerovich, Mark Grigorievich. *Kak vlast narod k trudu priuchala: zhilishche v SSSR – sredstvo upravleniia liudmi 1917–1941 gg (How the Government Trained the People to Work: Housing in the USSR as Means of People Management)*. Stuttgart: Ibidem-Verlag, 2005.

Mendel'son, V. 1937. "Kak popolnet'" (How to gain weight). *Obshchestvennitsa*, 16 (1937): 30–31.

Meyerhold, Meyerhold. "Akter budushchego" (Actor of the future), presentation in the Little Hall of the Conservatory, 12 May, 1922. RGALI, Fond 998, Opis 1.

Meyerhold, Vsevolod. Lectures in set design and biomechanics read in the first year of GVTYM in the school year 1921/1922, RGALI, Fond 998, Opis1, 738.

Meyerhold, Vsevolod. "Novy boi na teatralnom fronte" (The new battle on the theatrical front), speech read in Leningrad, 7 Jan. 1929. RGALI Fond 998, Opis1.

Meyerhold, Vsevolod. *Lektsii 1918–1919: Instruktorskie kursy, kursy masterstva stsenicheskikh postanovok, shkola akterskogo masterstva (Courses for Instructors, Courses in the Art of Set Design, a School of Actor's Art)*. Moscow: O.G.I., 2001.

Meyerhold, Vsevolod. Principles of Biomechanics. in a compilation of lectures written by students of GVTYM (Gosudarstvennye Vyshie Teatralnie Masterskie – State Higher Theatre Workshops) compiled by Korozhov, RGALI, Fond 998, Opis 1, Document 740, p. 42.

Milyutin, Nikolay A. *Sotsgorod: The Problem of Building Socialist Cities*, trans. Arthur Sprague. Cambridge, Mass.: MIT Press, 1974.

Morgan, George. "Luchshy' v mire" (Best in the world). In *Rasskazy stroitelei metro (Accounts of Metro Builders)*. Moscow: Istoriya fabrik i zavodov, 1935.

OBERIU group. "OBERIU Declaration." *Oxford Slavonic Papers, New Series*, III (1970): 69–73.

O' Mahoney, Mike. "Archaeological fantasies: Constructing history on the Moscow Metro." *The Modern Language Review* 98, no. 1 (Jan. 2003): 142.

Omarovich Khan-Magomedov, Selim. *Pioneers of Soviet Architecture: The Search for New Solutions in the 1920s and the 1930s*, trans. Alexander Lieven, ed. Catherine Cooke. London: Thames and Hudson, 1987.

Ostashevsky, Eugene, ed. *OBERIU: An Anthology of Russian Absurdism*. Evanston: Northwestern University Press, 2006: 83.

Ostrovskii, L.A. "Zhivaya lestnitsa" (The living stairway). In *Kak my stroili metro (How We Built the Metro)*. Moscow: Istoriya fabrik i zavodov, 1935.

Palmer, Scott W. *Dictatorship of the Air: Aviation Culture and the Fate of Modern Russia*. Cambridge: Cambridge University Press, 2006.

Paperny, Vladimir, *Architecture in the Age of Stalin: Culture Two*. Cambridge: Cambridge University Press, 2002.

Rammo, V. A. "Na poroge novogo bannogo stroitelstva" (On the threshold of new bathhouse construction). *Voprosy kommunalnogo khoziaistva* 1 (Jan. 1931): 47.

Randall, Amy. *The Soviet Dream: World of Retail Trade and Consumption in the 1930s*. London: Palgrave Macmillan, 2008.

Rappaport, Helen. *Joseph Stalin: A Biographical Companion*. Santa Barbara: ABC-Clio, 1999.

Reich, Wilhelm. *Sexual Revolution, and The Discovery of Orgone Vol. 1: The Function of the Orgasm*. New York: Orgone Institute Press, 1942.

Rohvarger, M. O. "Stantsiya Smolenskaya Ploshad'" (Station Smolensky Square). In *Kak my stroili metro*. Moscow: Istoriya fabrik i zavodov, 1935.

Semenova, T. M., "Istoriya proektirovaniya pervogo petrogradskogo krematoriya" (The history of designing the first petrograd crematorium). *Kraevedicheskie zapiski SPb – Issledovaniya i materialy* 4 (1996).

Siddiqi, Asif A. *The Red Rocket's Glare: Spaceflight and the Soviet Imagination, 1857–1957*. Cambridge: Cambridge University Press, 2010: 25–29.

Siegelbaum, Lewis H. *Soviet State and Society between Revolutions, 1918–1929*. Cambridge: Cambridge University Press, 1992.

Sloterdijk, Peter. "Cell block, egosphere, self-container: the apartment as a co-isolated existence" *Log* 10 (Summer/Fall 2007): 89–108.

Select bibliography 187

Smetenev, M. "*Novye mekhanicheskie prachechnye*" (New mechanical laundries). *Stroitelstvo Moskvy*, 6 (June 1930): 11–13

Smulevich, Boleslav Iakovlevich. *Materinstvo pri kapitalizme i socializme. (Motherhood in Capitalism and Socialism)*. Moscow: Gosudarstvennoe socialno-ekonomicheskoe izdatel'stvo, 1936.

Solomon R. Guggenheim Museum, State Tretyakov Gallery, State Russian Museum Schirn Kunsthalle Frankfurt. *The Great Utopia: Russian and Soviet Avant-garde, 1915–1932*. New York: Guggenheim Museum, 1992.

Stalin, Iosif Visaroionivich. "Speech at the First-Union Conference of Stakhanovites, November 17, 1935." In *Problems of Leninism*, Stalin, J.V., Peking: Foreign Language Press, 1976: 78.

Starostin, K. F. and others. "Bolsheviki na Metrostroie" (Bolsheviks of the Metrostroi). In *Kak my stroili metro*. Moscow: Istoriya fabrik i zavodov, 1935.

Stepanova, Varvara. "O rabotakh konstruktivistkoy molodezhi" (On the work of constructivist youth). *Lef* 3 (1923): 53.

Stites, Richard. *Revolutionary Dreams: Utopian Vision and Experimental Life in the Soviet Union*. Oxford: Oxford University Press, 1988.

Stovaratskii, A. "Zerkalo" (The mirror), from "Mama, Pochitai!" (Mother, read to me). *Obshchestvennitsa* 11 (1938): 55–56.

Strumilin, Stanislav. *Statistiko-ekonomicheskie etiudy (Studies in Statistics and Economics)*. Moscow-Leningrad: Planovoe khozaistvo, 1926.

Strumilin, Stanislav. *Problemy ekonomiki truda (Problems of Labor Economy)*. Moscow: Gosudarstvenoe izdatelstvo politicheskoi literatury, 1957.

Sushkin, G. "Oformlenie posadok" (The design of plantings). *Obshchestvennitsa* 8 (1937): 44–45.

Sushkin, G. "Tsvety i zelen na pervomayskikh torzhestvakh" (Flowers and greenery in the celebrations of the first of May). *Obshchestvennitsa* 6 (1937): 31.

Sushkin, G. "Vygonka rasteny" (Getting plants to open up). *Obshchestvennitsa* 21 (1937): 50.

Tafuri, Manfredo. *Architecture and Utopia*. Cambridge, Mass.: MIT Press, 1976.

Tafuri, Manfredo. *The Sphere and the Labyrinth*. Cambridge, Mass.: MIT Press, 1990.

Toporkov, Alexander. *Tehnichesky byt i sovremennoe isskustvo (Technical Everyday Life and Contemporary Art)*. Moscow and Leningrad: Gosudarstvennoe izdatelstvo, 1928.

Tsiolkovsky, Konstantin. *The Will of the Universe: Unknown Intelligence; Mind and Passions*, trans. Svetlana I. Zherebtsova. Moscow: Pamiat, 1992.

Volkov, Vadim, "The Concept of Kul'turnost': Notes on the Stalinist Civilizing Process." In *Stalinism – New Directions*, Sheila Fitzpatrick ed. London and New York: Routledge, 2000.

Udovički-Selb, Danilo. "Between modernism and socialist realism: Soviet architectural culture during Stalin's Revolution from Above, 1928–1938." *Journal of the Society of Architectural Historians* 68 no. 4 (Dec. 2009): 467–495.

Wheatcroft, S. G. "More light on the scale of repression and excess mortality in the Soviet Union in the 1930s." *Soviet Studies* 42, no. 2 (April 1990): 355–367.

Zhadova, Larissa Alekseevna, ed. *Tatlin*. New York: Rizzoli, 1989.

Zoshchenko, Mikhail. *Scenes From the Bathhouse, and Other Stories of Communist Russia*, trans. Sidney Monas, ed. Marc Slonim. Ann Arbor: University of Michigan Press, 1962.

Index

Notes are indicated by an 'n'. For example, 121n.6 refers to note 6 on page 121.
Page numbers in italics refer to a figure on that page.

abortion 125–6
aeroplanes 18–28
　heroic mythology 18, 26–8
　poetry 21
　Russian futurists 18–21
　Tatlin and 22–6
alcoholism 98–9
Althusser, Louis 8n.9
architecture
　bathhouses 97–120
　citizens' transfiguration by 33
　domestic 65–96
　as materialist art 77
　Moscow Metro 155–76
　productivist vs. representational 4–5, 120
　Soviet context 1–6, 177–9
　theatre 4–5, 37–64
arkhitektons 114
art
　avant-garde and Stalinism 144–50
　cultural–political change and 1–2
　painting 135–9
　see also architecture; socialist realism; theatre
Arvatov, Boris 49–50, 70–3
Association of Real Art (OBERIU) 91
avant-garde
　Arvatov and 70
　capitalism and 8n.7
　cultural–political change and 1–2
　enthusiasm for aviation 21
　furniture 73–8, 85, 88
　Stalinism an extension of 144–50
　textures 167–9

Bakhtin, Mikhail 61n.1
Balmas-Neary, Rebecca 151n.5
banya *see* bathhouses
Barshch, Mikhail 81–5
bathhouses 97–120
　availability 121n.6
　bather as 'product' 106–7
　classical references in 107
　communal laundries and 102–5
　crematoriums and 107–9
　descriptions 98–100
　history 97–102
　as microcosm of communism 109, 120
　mysticism and 115–20
　Nikolsky and 109–20
　recycling in 108–9
　state control 102
beauty and fashion 127–9
Benjamin, Walter 162
bioenergetics 41
biomechanics 38, 40, 45–60, 70–2
Bogdanov, Alexander 15–18, 42
Bolsheviks 43
bourgeoisie 43–4, 126
Buchlow, Benjamin 7n.4

byt (the everyday) 19–21, 24, 29, 30, 33, 49–50
bytie (spiritual existence) 19–21, 33

capitalism 2, 14, 33, 143
Central Institute of Labour (TsIT) 21, 24, 40–1
Chaplin, Charlie 53
Chechulin, Dmitry 164
children 125–6, 131, 133, 146–8
Chkalov, Valery 27
chronotope 37–8
Clark, Katerina 4, 9n.11
class *see* bourgeoisie; working class
collectivization 81–6, 162
communes 78, 81–7
communism *see* Marxism; socialism
Communist Party 44, 125
cosmist movement 14–18
  see also futurists
cosmonauts 28–33
crematoriums 107–9
Crommelynck, Fernand 37, 50
Culture and Everyday Life (journal) 98–9, 102

Deleuze, Gilles 8n.9, 60
Demkov, Nikolay *105*, 121n.5
dialectical materialism 34n.16
disurbanist movement 87–91
divorce 125
Dobrenko, Evgeny 4, 9n.12, 133, 143
domestic life *see* home life; housing; women
Dom Narkomfin (commune) 78, 81
Dushkin, Alexey 164–5

El Lissitsky 7n.5, 111–14

family
  destruction intended 85–6
  differing lifestyles 78
  women and 132–3, 135–6
fashion and beauty 127–9
Fedorov, Nikolay 14
fiction 14–18
Fitzpatrick, Sheila 125

Five-Year Plans 3, 99, 101, 102, 107, 155, 156, 162
food 130–4
Fordism 40, 44
Foucault, Michel 8n.9
Frankfurt Kitchen 78–9
furniture 73–8, 85, 88
futurists 18–21
  see also cosmist movement

Gagarin, Yuri 28–9
Gastev, Aleksey
  'cyclograms' by 24–5
  Marxism and 43, 44
  proletarian as machine 14–15, 38–42, 45–6, 57–8
  Strumilin and 68
  Taylorism and 40–1
  workers' transcendence 59–60
Gegello, Alexander 106–9
Ginzburg, Moisei 168–9
Goldenberg, N. A. 101
Gorky, Maxim 156
Gortseridze, I. D. 165
GosPlan 65
Gray, Boris 8n.6
Great Famine 131
Gronsky, Ivan 135
Groys, Boris 144
Guattari, Felix 8n.9, 60
Guggenheim Museum 31
Gundorov, N. I. 121n.5

Harms, Danil 91–2
Hays, Michael 61n.1
Higher Artistic-Technical Institute (VKhuTeIn) 73
home life 65–96
  collectivization of 81–6
  communist identity and 92–3
  domestic objects of 68–73
  family in 85
  furniture in 73–8, 85, 88
  leisure time in 65–8
  things as co-workers 70–2
  see also housing; women
horticulture 137–9

Index

housing
  collectivization 81–6
  disurbanist movement 87–91
  eligibility 78
  living space 77–8
Hudson, Hugh 6n.2
humanism 76–7
hunger 130, 131, 132

immortality 14–15, 16
Individual House No. 30 87–91
INKhUK (Institute for Artistic Culture) 114
Institute for Artistic Culture (INKhUK) 114
interior decoration 135–7
Italian futurism 21

Kabakov, Ilya 30–3
Kaganovich, Lazar 157, 158, 162–3, 164
Kamensky, Vasily 18–21
Kiaer, Kristina 7n.4, 93n.6
kitchens 78–82
Krasin, Leonid 14
Kravets, S. M. 167
Krichevsky, David 107–9
Kudryakov, Ivan 98–9

labour
  culture of movement and 53–6
  eroticisation of 39–40, 46–7, 58–60
  immortality and 14–15
  machines as co-workers 41–2
  Marx on 43
  proletarian consciousness and 41–2
  Taylorism and 40–1, 44–5, 46, 50, 57–8
  theatrical interpretation 45–61
Lacan, Jacques 8n.9
Ladinsky, Anatoly 117–20
laundries, industrial 102–5
Law, Alma 53
Le Corbusier 21, 74, 87–8
leisure time 65–8
Leningrad Trust for Public Baths and Laundries 97

Leninism 3–4, 43, 44, 99
Leonov, Aleksey 28–9
Letatlin (flying machine) 22–6
Likhtenberg, Yakov 164–5
Lilienthal, Otto 24

"The Magnanimous Cuckold" (play) 37–8, 53–8
Malevich, Kazimir 114
marriage 125–6
Mars 'exploration' 14–18
Marxism 43, 45, 86
"Maxim Gorky" (aeroplane) 27
Meerovich, Mark 77–8
Melnikov, Konstantin 111
Meyerhold, Vsevolod
  biomechanical approach of 48–9
  chronotope of 37–8
  Gastev and 46–8, 58–60
  set design 55–8
  theatre as production 50–6, 120
  theatrical world-machine 58–60
Milyutin, Nikolay 85–6
Modernism
  aeroplanes 18–28
  bathhouses 97–120
  home life 65–96
  housing 72–91
  Moscow Metro 155–73
  the Soviet woman 125–54
  space flight 11–18, 28–33
  theatre 37–64
Morgan, George 174n.5
Moscow 156, 162
Moscow Metro 150, 155–76
  aesthetic 'superiority' 163–7
  city planning and 162–3
  construction 155–6
  as 'cosmetic' project 150
  materials 165–9
  opening 158–9
  popular acculturation 169–73
  propaganda 155–9
  socialist modernity and 159–61, 173
  technical inferiority 164
  textures 167–9
Mrsakov 116–17

Muravev, Valerian 14–15

New Economic Policy 99
Nikolsky, Alexander 109–20
　El Lissitzky and 111–14
　mysticism of 115–20
　Orthodox references of 109–10,
　　111, 119
　projects 110–13
NKVD 78

OBERIU (Association of Real Art) 91
Obshchestvennitsa (women's magazine)
　artistic education 134–9
　background 126–7
　communist beauty 127–9
　defence of the USSR 145–50
　interior decoration 139–44
　nutrition 130–4
　sex life 125–6
　women's activism 138–44, 148–50
October Revolution 1, 2
Okhitovich, Mikhail 87
Ordzhonikidze, Grigory 127
OSA (Organization of Contemporary Architects) 87–8

painting 134–9
Paperny, Vladimir 9n.10–11
peasants 78
Piranesi, Battista 8n.7
Plastov, Arkady 133–4
Popova, Lyubov 51, 54–6
Population 131–2
post-structuralism 3
Pravda 26, 27, 39
Problems of Municipal Economy (*Voprosy komunalnogo khozyaystva*) 102, 107
production *see* labour
propaganda
　How We Built the Metro 157–8, 163–4, 167, 170–2
　Obshchestvennitsa magazine 125–50
　Stories of Metro Builders 156, 161–2
　USSR in Construction (*SSSR na stroike*) 113–14, 127
psychotechnics 41

Ranciere, Jacques 8n.9
Randall, Amy 152n.6
Rebrov (Brigadier) 155
recycling 108–9
Red Fleet 26–8
Reich, Wilhelm 60
Rubens, Peter Paul 128–9, 135
Russian Revolution 1, 2

Schütte-Lihotzky, Margarete 79
Schvester, Vera 127
science fiction 14–18
Slezkin, Yuri 125
Sobolev, Nikolay 75
Social Democrats 43
social engineering 41
socialism
　aeroplanes and 18–28
　bathhouses and 97–120
　home life 65–96
　housing 72–91
　Moscow Metro 155–73
　productivist vs. representational theories 3–5, 120
　space flight and 11–18, 28–33
　theatre and 4–5, 37–64
　utopian visions and 1–2, 13–21, 77
　women and 125–54
　see also Marxism; Stalinism
socialist realism
　bathhouses and 120
　economy of 143–4
　painting and 134–9
　women and 133–9, 142–4
Soviet New Man 2–6, 177–9
　see also socialism; Stalinism; women; working class
Soviet Union
　defence 27–8
　famine 131
　reorganization of production 44–5
Sovremennaya arkhitektura (*Contemporary Architecture*) 73, 78–81, *82*, 87
space travel 11–18, 28–33
　cosmonauts 28–33
　socialist utopias and 14–18
　Tsiolkovsky and 11–14, 28
SSSR na stroike (*USSR in Construction*) 113–14

Index

Stalinism 125–54
  as aesthetic project 2, 144, 150
  cultural trends under 1–2
  extension of avant-garde 144–50
  as perversion of freedom 1, 179
  productivist vs. representational theories 3–5, 120, 133, 144–5
  propaganda 125–54
  Stalin as collective father 125–6, 133
Stites, Richard 6n.1
Stroitel 122n.13
Strumilin, Stanislav
  Arvatov and 70
  domestic object studies 68–73
  Gastev and 68
  Individual House No. 30 87
  leisure time studies 65–8
suprematist movement 114
Sushkin, G. 137–9

Tafuri, Manfredo 8n.7
Tatlin, Vladimir 22–6, 33, 73
Taylorism 40–1, 44–5, 46, 50, 57–8, 103, 107
Tereshkova, Valentina 28–9
theatre
  "The Magnanimous Cuckold" 37–8, 53–8
  Meyerhold and 37–8, 46–9
  as production 50–2
  proletarian identity and 38, 46–9
Toporkov, Alexander 73–7, 91
Trotsky, Noah 101
Tsiolkovsky, Konstantin 11–14, 28
TsIT (Central Institute of Labour) 21, 24, 40–1

Udovički-Selb, Danilo 7n.5
Ukraine 131
United States 72, 76
USSR in Construction (SSSR na stroike) 113–14, 127

Veber, H. 121n.7
Verne, Jules 12
Vesnin brothers 111
VKhuTeIn (Higher Artistic-Technical Institute) 73
VKhUTEMAS (constructivist group) 70, 81, 88
Vladimirov, Vladimir 81–5
Volkov, Vadim 176n.40
Voprosy komunalnogo khozyaystva (Problems of Municipal Economy) 102, 107
Vostok 1 28

women 125–54
  activism of 126–9, 137, 138–44, 148–50
  beauty and fashion 127–9
  diet 131–4
  'fabricating' the world 139–44
  horticulture and 137–9
  interior decoration and 135–7
  military role 145, 148–50
  motherhood 125–6, 132–3, 145–8
  sex lives 125–6
  socialist realism and 133–9, 142–4
  Stalinist paternalism 125–6, 133
working class
  acculturation 169–73
  aeroplanes and 22–6
  creation of 4, 5, 43–5
  eroticisation of 39–40, 46–7, 58–60
  ideal worker 155
  as machine 38–42, 45–8, 57–8
  rejecting communes 78
  theatrical performance and 38, 46–9, 51, 58–9

Yezhova, Yevgeniya 127

Zoshchenko, Mikhail 98–9

EU authorised representative for GPSR:
Easy Access System Europe, Mustamäe tee 50,
10621 Tallinn, Estonia
gpsr.requests@easproject.com

www.ingramcontent.com/pod-product-compliance
Lightning Source LLC
Chambersburg PA
CBHW070238240426
43673CB00044B/1844